Turning THE *Tide*

Confronting the Money Traders

BY JOHN DILLON
ECUMENICAL COALITION FOR ECONOMIC JUSTICE

Canadian Centre for Policy Alternatives

PRINTED IN CANADA

Acknowledgments

We gratefully acknowledge the contributions that a number of individuals and organizations made to this publication.

We wish to thank the Public Service Alliance of Canada and InterPares for their financial support.

This book is co-published by the Ecumenical Coalition for Economic Justice and the Canadian Centre for Policy Alternatives. Thanks to Ed Finn, Bruce Campbell and Diane Touchette of the CCPA for their many hours of work editing, designing and laying out this publication.

We appreciate the many contributions from our friends in Mexico without whom Chapter Four could not have been written. To Alberto Arroyo, Andres Penaloza, Alejandro Alvarez, Mario Monroy, Victor Osorio and Bertha Lujan muchas gracias.

Although John Dillon did most of the writing, the writing of this publication is, as always, a joint effort by the ECEJ staff and administrative committee. Lorraine Michael, Mark Hathaway and Geoffrey Johnston made substantial contributions to the text. Other members of the ECEJ administrative committee and staff, particularly Jennifer Wershler Henry, Barbara Paleczny, David Pfrimmer, Lee McKenna-Ducharme, Doryne Kirby, Joy Kennedy and Bernard Dufresne contributed suggestions for the content and made invaluable comments on various drafts. Diana Gibbs assisted in steering this book through the publication process.

Many friends of ECEJ kindly gave comments on earlier drafts. We wish particularly to thank Jim Stanford of the Canadian Auto Workers for his astute observations and suggestions.

Contents

CHAPTER ONE
Symptoms of Global Disorder

"Speculation may do no harm as bubbles on a steady stream of enterprise. But the position is serious when enterprise becomes the bubble on a whirlpool of speculation."

—John Maynard Keynes

Increasingly, our economy is becoming divorced from reality. The activities which generate the highest monetary returns often have little or no real value. They neither sustain nor enhance life, and may even destroy it. Some activities which are truly productive, like caring for children, yield little in the way of money. Speculators earn millions buying and selling contracts for currencies or commodities that will never be delivered. Meanwhile, peasant women struggling to nurture the soil and their families are condemned to poverty.

Over the past two decades, the world economy has entered a radically new phase. World markets for capital, goods and services are increasingly integrated. New technologies are displacing human labour at an alarming rate. Economic growth leaves millions of unemployed workers without secure jobs, because such "growth" is measured only as an increase in the money economy. Industrial employers are no longer concerned with paying their employees enough to buy the products they make.

Stock markets sag on news of rising employment, and share prices often rise after firms announce layoffs. Investment is shifting from the production of goods and services to financial speculation.

Taken together, these phenomena—globalization, technological change, the abandonment of the local market, and increasing speculation—constitute a new stage of capitalism. Although all these factors are important, we focus in this study on the power of financial capital. Finance is no longer just a means of facilitating the exchange of goods and services. Rather, it has become a dominant force shaping peoples' destinies.

Speculation Growing

The financial economy has grown to nearly incomprehensible proportions. Every day, about US$1.3 trillion worth of currencies change hands on world markets.[1] The vast majority of these transactions are speculative. When the famous British economist John Maynard Keynes first warned against the danger of finance dominating the real economy, financial exchanges were about twice as large as merchandise trade. Today financial transactions are **seventy-two times** as large as merchandise trade.[2]

However, foreign exchange trading only accounts for about one-quarter of the speculative economy. When the markets for currencies, stocks, bonds and commodity futures are taken together, **daily transactions total some US$ 4 trillion**. Most of these transactions are speculative; they are not in and of themselves necessary to finance the production or trade of goods and services.

The Bank for International Settlements estimates that the pool of "hot money" that can flow instantaneously around the world through telecommunications networks amounts to US$13 trillion.[3]

Other indicators of the explosive growth of international financial wheeling and dealing include:

- an estimated US$2.5 trillion worth of tradable securities (bonds and stocks) are held outside their country of origin;
- the stock of net international bank loans rose to US$4.2 trillion in 1994, up from US$265 billion in 1975;
- the value of international bonds rose to US$2 trillion in 1994 from US$259 billion in 1982.[4]

Cybermoney

Most transactions in today's financial economy take place through the electronic exchange of money, allowing vast sums to move around the globe in seconds. Throughout history money, as a socially recognized means of storing and exchanging wealth, has taken many forms including live cattle, beads, precious metals, and playing cards.

Money has been somewhat of an abstraction ever since the invention of paper currency. In today's world, though, stores of wealth no longer take the form of printed bank notes or pieces of gilded paper that represent bonds and stock certificates. Instead, vast fortunes are visible only on computer screens as what might be called "cybermoney". Most of these "assets" are really just digital electronic information moving between computerized accounts. They only exist by social convention.

Financial instruments are worth something only as long as people maintain confidence in the system. When multi-million-dollar financial transactions take place over telecommunications networks, nothing tangible changes hands. Nevertheless, speculators grow very wealthy doing nothing more tangible than rearranging zeroes and ones on computer chips as they buy and sell cybermoney. Meanwhile, much of what is truly valuable, that which sustains human life and natural ecosystems, is treated as valueless unless it can be bought and sold as a commodity.

COUNTING THE COST

The old industrial capitalism of the post-war years has been replaced by a new, meaner, finance-centered capitalism. It is often more profitable to speculate on financial instruments such as commodity futures, currency contracts and derivatives (in essence, as we will see in Chapter 2, sophisticated ways of gambling) than to invest in the production of goods and services.

Speculation brings greater returns—at least according to the way we have grown accustomed to measuring these things—than does real work.

When investors build factories, buy machines and hire workers to produce a product or a service, the real economy is said to expand. When investors multiply their profits by trading in financial assets, or just collect interest on bonds, the financial economy grows. In this new stage of capitalism there is no longer a commitment to full employment and enhanced social welfare.

As Frank Stronach, owner of Magna Corporation, once put it: "Why

Chart One
Nominal and Real Prime Interest Rates in Canada
1974 to Third Quarter 1996

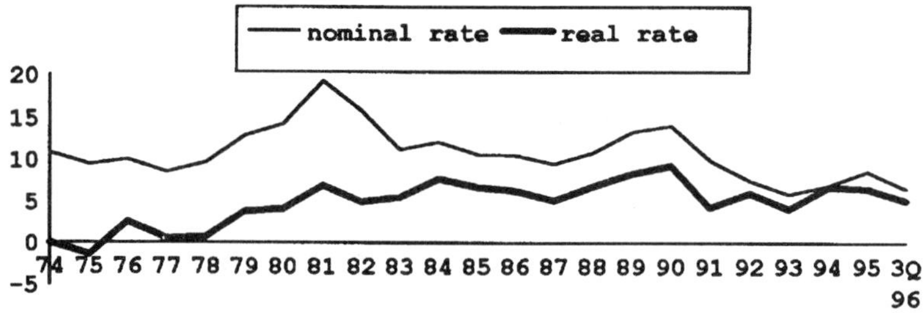

Source: Department of Finance Economic Tables and Bank of Canada Review

would you pour a foundation, buy machines, hire employees if you can make as much money buying bonds?”[5] Not surprisingly, the extremely high relative growth of the speculative economy has resulted in rising unemployment. Over the period 1950-1980, the average rate of unemployment, as officially measured by Statistics Canada, was 5.3%. During the last 15 years (1981-1995), unemployment has averaged 9.8%. In the first half of 1996, unemployment officially averaged 9.6%. This figure does not include nearly half a million “discouraged workers” who have given up looking for work, and the one-third of part-time workers who want, but cannot find, full-time employment.

Combined with stagnant real wages, rising unemployment has been one of the principal causes of an increasingly unjust distribution of wealth in Canada and throughout the world. This new era of speculative capitalism is increasing income disparities at an alarming rate. In 1981, the richest 20% of Canadians earned 19 times as much as the poorest 20% before taxes and social transfers. By 1994, the wealthiest quintile earned **24 times as much** as the poorest 20%.[6] A prime reason why the richest group prospered after 1981 was because their investment income was buoyed by high interest rates.

The misery of the unemployed and the wealth accumulated by financial investors are directly related. The Bank of Canada, our central bank, deliberately pursues policies that keep unemployment high as a means of curtailing inflation. The principal beneficiaries of these policies are financial investors who profit from high real (that is, inflation-adjusted) interest rates.

Although nominal interest rates came down during 1996, real rates remain well above their historical levels. The nominal prime rate for the first three-quarters of 1996 averaged 6.5%. With inflation running at 1.4% over the same period, the real prime rate is (6.5 - 1.4) 5.1%, which is more than three times as high as the average real rate of 1.5% over the period 1935 to 1984. As Chart One shows, while nominal interest rates have declined from their peak in 1981, real interest rates have remained very high throughout the 1980s and 1990s.

Internationally, income polarization has also increased dramatically. Prior to 1980, the gap between the rich and the poor grew because the rich were becoming wealthier faster than the poor improved their lot. Since 1980, the rich have not only become more affluent, but the poor have become poorer in absolute rather than just relative terms.

Chart Two
Ratio of income disparity between the richest and the poorest 20% of the world's population

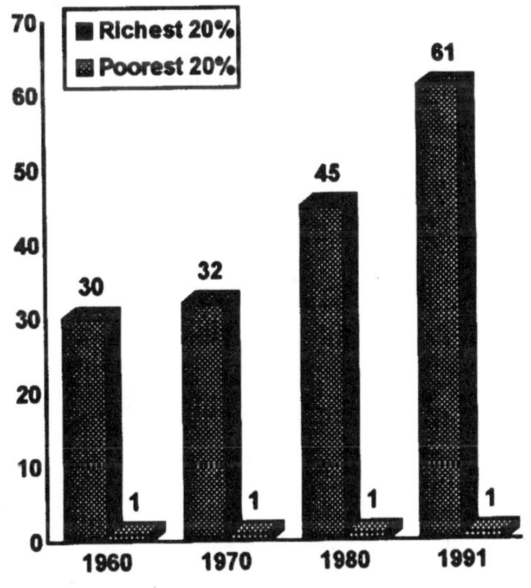

Source: United Nations Development Program

On an income per capita basis in 1960, the wealthiest one-fifth of the world's population received **30 times** more than the poorest 20%. By 1991, the most affluent one-fifth had become **61 times** wealthier than the poorest quintile.[7]

These figures only measure average per capita incomes in developed and less developed countries. When the wealth gap within countries is taken into account, the richest 20% of the world's people are **150 times** more affluent than the poorest 20%. In 1994, just 358 individuals had personal fortunes worth US$762 billion. These billionaires' wealth was as large as the income of the poorest 45% of the world's population, some 2.3 billion people.[8]

Some 30% of the world's labour force, representing 820 million people, are counted as unemployed by the International Labour Organization.

Most official data on employment and income distribution ignore the contribution made by women's unpaid work in the home and in subsistence agriculture. For the high rollers of world finance, people are becoming less important—both as producers and as consumers. Latin Americans no longer speak about the millions who live in absolute poverty as the "marginalized," since this term implies that sooner or later they might be incorporated into the mainstream of society. Instead they now speak about "the excluded" masses who neither produce for the world economy nor consume from it. In Colombia the excluded have even been described as "the disposable ones".[9]

Natural and Sustenance Economy Undermined

While only a small portion of humanity actually profits from the new economy, the costs are widely dispersed. Speculative activities essentially create money without producing anything of intrinsic value. So what does such money actually represent? In effect, it is a lien against future production. As Herman Daly and John Cobb note in their book, <u>For the Common Good:</u>

> Money balances do not imply the existence of any real goods at all. The willingness of the community to hold money derives from the inconvenience of barter, and the fact that money is an indent or lien against *future* production, which cannot spoil because it does not yet exist. But the real wealth of the community, even in a money economy, consists of goods to which the principle of spoilage still applies. So accumulating money balances cannot indefinitely be matched by accumulating real wealth. Therefore at some point accumulated money becomes a lien against future production rather than a claim check to simultaneously existing goods. The willingness of future producers to honor those past claims on their current production will at some point become an issue.[10]

As the financial economy continues to accumulate immense balances of money, its claims against future production also grow. Not surprisingly, then, the global financial economy is pushing aside two other economies that traditionally nurture and give life. As Vandana Shiva observes: "Nature's economy (through which environmental regeneration takes place) and the people's sustenance economy (within which women produce the sustenance for society through 'invisible' unpaid work) are being systematically destroyed to create growth in the global market economy."[11]

The world of money and finance operates according to a different logic from the world of nature and daily life, where women perform most of the useful activities—gardening, cooking, house cleaning, child care, etc.—that sustain life. The money system presumes that growth must go on incessantly. In order to pay interest on past debt, there must be continuous expansion of remunerative activity. Otherwise the whole pyramid would collapse.

But endless expansion is not natural. Living organisms can only grow so large before they become dysfunctional. We identify uncontrolled growth with cancer. Nor is unlimited growth ecologically sustainable. Some ecosystems have already reached their limits as resources are consumed faster than they can be replaced.

Free trade deals like the North American Free Trade Agreement (NAFTA) are designed to allow an affluent minority of the world's population to have access to a disproportionate share of the remaining non-renewable natural resources. This moneyed minority enjoys lifestyles based on imported raw materials that could not be sustained by using local resources alone. The richest fifth now consume roughly 80% of the world's resources, while the poorest lack the bare necessities.

The Erosion of the Power of Governments

Why don't democratically elected governments intervene to control the depredation wrought by speculative capitalism? Are governments powerless to act, or is it that they choose not to?

In a remarkable speech delivered to a group of former heads of government, Prime Minister Jean Chrétien recently spoke about how dependence on international finance is eroding the power of nation states. He acknowledged how "a sense of not being able to control our economic destiny [...] adds to the general anxiety about job security, our standard of living, and the world our children will inherit."

The Prime Minister described how "international finance knows no borders. Tidal waves of money wash effortlessly backwards and forwards, buffeting interest rates and exchange rates [and disrupting] the best-laid plans of governments. These financial waves often seem motivated by quick-changing sentiments or the short-term expectations of the proverbial 28-year-old trader in red suspenders. When a crisis erupts, a nation state can seem powerless."[12]

While we appreciate Mr. Chrétien's candid description, we do not accept his conclusions. The Prime Minister argues that states can influence financial flows but cannot control them. He concludes that "We cannot stop globalization. We need to [...] adjust to it."[13] But adjusting to global financial markets means that governments have to adopt the monetary and fiscal policies demanded by wealthy investors. These financiers demand that governments fight the spectre of inflation through high interest rates and high unemployment, and cut spending to reduce their deficits.

In essence, ***this implies that democratically elected governments must abdicate their responsibility for promoting an economy which benefits all their citizens.***

If financiers demand that governments fight the spectre of inflation through high real interest rates so as to guarantee the profitability of their investments, governments must do so even though the cost is higher unemployment and growing despair.

Mr. Chrétien calls for appeasing the global financiers by keeping public finances "in good shape." This means continuing to battle deficits through spending cuts rather than addressing their actual causes by reforming taxation or adopting a different monetary policy. The Prime Minister says that "restoring our fiscal health and regaining our fiscal flexibility [...] will allow us to channel our scarce financial resources to the people that need them most."[14] In fact, the high real interest rates, high unemployment, and austerity policies demanded by the financial markets are taking us in the opposite direction. They are channeling resources **away** from people who need them most, while enriching those who are already wealthy.

Is there no other way? Is it true that we cannot escape from the power of international financiers? Certainly, we must recognize the reality of the power they wield. But we do not accept Mr. Chrétien's contention that we must adjust to the demands of financial capital. On the contrary, we believe that, if we try to play by the rules set by the financiers, we risk everything we hold sacred: our social programs, the integrity of our environment, and even our compassion and our humanity.

The purpose of this book is to show that we have other options. We intend to probe more deeply than Mr. Chrétien dared to go. We shall explore the links between the globalization of finance and growing poverty and unemployment. We shall show that we need not be ruled by the power of global financiers.

An Ethical Choice

The endless pursuit of cybermoney is a type of idolatry, the worship of a false god. Although greed and usury are as old as the earliest biblical writings condemning them, the current era of speculative capitalism has elevated money worship to a new plateau. Whereas we believe that the financial system should serve the enhancement of human life and the natural environment, the era of speculative capitalism has transformed it into a destructive force.

David Korten sums up the problem: "The more the money world becomes globalized, the more the links between the living world and the money world become tenuous ... the more the money system predominates." The challenge we face is to bring control back to the local level, so that the financial system is guided by people "whose view of reality is not shaped entirely by the numbers they see on their computer screens as they trade shares, stock options and derivatives."[15]

The first step to bringing back control to the people is to try to understand the workings of the financial economy. In this introduction we have described only a few symptoms of the unhealthy state of the world economy. In the next three chapters we shall expand the diagnosis. Some of the concepts we shall introduce will be new to some readers. We'll do our best to explain them as clearly as we can. Even though some may find these concepts difficult to understand, we need to learn more about the world of global finance if we are to challenge the forces misshaping our world.

In Chapter Two we shall examine the growing power of the money traders over decisions that should rest with democratically elected governments. Chapter Three will look at how Canada is particularly vulnerable to speculative capital flows. The fourth chapter will explore the role that hot money played in Mexico's financial crisis and show how NAFTA is prolonging that crisis.

The final chapter will explore what can be done at the international, national and local levels to challenge speculative capitalism and develop viable alternatives.

CHAPTER TWO

The Parasitic Phase of Capitalism

Two Lives - Two Worlds

Gabriela is a peasant farmer and the mother of five children living in the Andean highlands of South America. She works long hours to care for her family, her animals, and her land. Every day, she makes numerous trips to the stream at the bottom of a steep hill to fetch heavy pails of water. She cuts wood, tends the fire, and cooks. She also helps care for the family's crops of potatoes, wheat, and quinoa, and raises small animals and a few sheep.

Gabriela is normally engaged in numerous activities at the same time. Even when she is conversing with a neighbor, she is spinning wool by hand or knitting. She is constantly tending to the youngest child strapped to her back. For Gabriela, there are no holidays. She loves her land, its plants, and the animals she raises. She nurtures them as she does her own family. She creates and cultivates many things of value; yet, she is very poor.

Life has always been hard for Gabriela, but in recent years things have become even more difficult. The food that she sells in town has actually fallen in price as cheaper imports have flooded the local market. At the same time, the cost of agricultural supplies, health care, and schooling have risen steeply. While several of her own children have been able to go to primary school (requiring immense sacrifices by her and her husband), she worries that, in the face of rising prices for books and school supplies, her youngest daughter may never attend classes.

Gabriela's oldest daughter, Juanita, left home a year ago to work in a clothing factory in a city on the coast. She sends a small sum of money home every month, something which helps the family make ends meet. Still, Gabriela is worried about the long hours and difficult living conditions her daughter must endure. She had always hoped life would be better for her children than herself, but she now fears that they may be even poorer.

- - -

John works as a trader for a large Toronto bank. He earns a six-figure income and has accumulated significant personal investments of his own. John rises early and turns on his home computer to check the overnight action on the Asian and European markets before going in to work. He works alongside other traders in a room with a special air-conditioning system. It keeps the computers from overheating and pumps extra oxygen into the room to keep the traders alert.

He carefully analyzes all the latest market trends to make profitable investments for his bank. He uses sophisticated mathematical formulas and a high-speed computer programmed to spot price differentials faster than any human could.

During market hours, John sits in front of his computer executing trades in a number of North American bond markets. It's stressful work, but also thrilling and challenging. His colleagues specialize in other financial instruments such as derivatives, interest rate futures, and commodity markets. Together, they make up a highly skilled team who generate millions of dollars in yearly earnings for their employer.

John is basically an honest man. He plays by the rules of the game. He laughs at the stereotype of "the boys in red suspenders," which he never wears. He'd like to spend time in community activities, but finds he has little extra time given his stressful work schedule. Still, he's able to spend some time with his family each day. He hopes that, in a few more years, he can win a promotion to a managerial position before he burns out.

- - -

At first glance, John and Gabriela seem to live in completely different worlds, and in some sense that is true. Yet, their activities are not unrelated. The trades that John and his colleagues execute in the world's financial markets in some way affect Gabriela. The pressure exerted by international money markets has resulted in the structural adjustment policies that have raised the cost of education and health care for Gabriela's family.

Trading in commodities and pressure for "open markets" affect the price of food imports and agricultural supplies, pushing Gabriela's income down. Gabriela is affected by the global market and the decisions of people like John, yet she has no control or voice in the direction of the world economy.

No one would doubt that Gabriela's activities are valuable. What could be more fundamental to the sustenance of life than the production of food and the care of children? Yet she receives little or no monetary remuneration for this work. In the eyes of the global economy, what she does is virtually worthless.[16]

John, on the other hand, produces nothing of intrinsic worth. His activities are basically speculative, analogous in some ways to gambling. True, he works hard and employs considerable skill and expertise. There is no evidence that he desires to harm people like Gabriela. Yet, in the end, many of his activities prove destructive when seen from the perspective of actually enhancing the quality of life. Despite this, he is rewarded handsomely. He is considered a valued player in the global economy.

A Question of Values

For most people in the technological world of the North, economics is seen as the "art" of making money. From this perspective, the growth of speculative finance seems to be just a new and more efficient phase of the game of making money. Players like John can make large profits. Those who are unable to get into the game will lose out.

But is making money what economics is really about? How can we say that speculative activities "create wealth" when nothing of real value is ever produced? And what of the cost in terms of rising unemployment, growing disparities of wealth, and ecological destruction?

Questions of economics are, ultimately, questions of value. What value do we assign to activities and resources? These are, at heart, ethical questions, despite the fact that modern economics is presented as a science, divorced from considerations of morality.

We often forget that the root meaning of economics, or its Greek equivalent, "oikonomia", means "the care and management of the household." In other words, when we speak of economics we should be speaking of the care and management of our home, our community, our world. From our values perspective, we view economics as the art of sustaining and enhancing life itself. This is even clearer when we see that "economics" and "ecology" are both derived from the same root.

Aristotle made a clear distinction between economics (oikonomia) and purely speculative activity which produced nothing of real value. He called the latter set of activities "chrematistics," which can be defined as "the branch of political economy relating to the manipulation of property and wealth so as to maximize short-term monetary exchange value to the owner."[17]

Aristotle's classic example of chrematistics concerned the philosopher Thales of Miletus. When the local citizens chided Thales for his simple lifestyle—saying in effect that his philosophy was obviously useless because he had accumulated no wealth through it—Thales took up their challenge. Through his knowledge of astronomy, he was able to predict a bumper olive harvest. While winter still lay over the land, he leased all the olive presses in the area at a bargain price. When harvest time came, he was able to make huge monopoly profits.

Thales employed chrematistics to his advantage. The difference between him and the modern-day chrematists engaged in speculative capitalism is that he saw his activities in their true light: as little more than a cheap trick to extract profit at the expense of others. "After all, Thales had planted no olive trees, built no olive presses, discovered no new uses for olive oil, and made no one but himself better off."[18]

Speculative Capitalism: The New Chrematistics

The world of speculative capitalism is fundamentally an exercise in chrematistics. Like Thales and his olive presses, financial assets are often generated without creating anything of real value. The money thus accumulated is a claim against the future production of real goods. Attempts to generate enough surplus to pay back that money often result in the destructive "mining" of ecosystems and the unjust exploitation of human labour.

In an earlier era, those who profited from investments without engaging in useful production were called "rentiers". The term, borrowed from the French language, refers to those who collect "rent" from their ownership of land or other assets without having to work for it. Interest on loans may be thought of as a form of rent paid for the use of money. Rentier incomes are often higher than the normal return that might be earned on capital invested in production.

Strictly speaking, a speculator is not the same thing as a rentier. A speculator makes money by betting on the **direction** of price movements. Thus a speculator can make money even when prices are falling by taking a "short" position, that is, selling commodities or financial instruments for future delivery.

Classic rentier behavior is somewhat different from the actions of today's financial elite. A classic rentier would hold on to the title to his or her bonds until they reached maturity. Today's speculators may only hold a market position for a few minutes, hours or days before selling again on highly volatile, computerized markets.

The Ethics of Making Money from Money

Societal attitudes to the ethics of interest-taking and rentier behavior have evolved over time. Up until the Middle Ages, the Church maintained the biblical prohibition against taking interest on loans. Gradually the notion of usury was redefined to mean the taking of **excessive** interest payments, although the definition of "excessive" is hard to pin down. In the accompanying box we explain how John Calvin's thinking had a major influence on the evolution of European attitudes to interest-taking.

In the morality of the early days of capitalism, rentiers were despised as unproductive parasites. John Ralston Saul cites Adam Smith in this regard:

"As soon as the land of any country has all become private property, the landlords, like all other men, love to reap what they have never sowed, and demand a rent even for its natural produce... Wherever capital predominates, industry prevails; wherever revenue, idleness."[19]

In his insightful book on *Economics in Crisis*, Louis-Philippe Rochon observes that classical economists like David Ricardo viewed the basic conflict in society as between capitalists and rentiers, and not the class struggle between capitalists and workers, as Karl Marx maintained. Rochon asserts that "the most important development in our economy in the last 15 years has been the resurgence of the rentiers and their control over a large part of the economy."[20]

Today's rentiers seek to profit from their financial investments by using their political and financial power to maintain high real (that is, inflation-adjusted) interest rates and unregulated financial markets. The rentiers' political power stems from their ability to withhold finance from governments whom they deem to be pursuing "unwise" policies.

As we shall see in the discussion of monetary policy to follow, bond traders can bid up interest rates through the sale of government bonds. The losers are the unemployed, genuine entrepreneurs who would invest in production, and middle-income taxpayers who pay for the cost of servicing government debts at higher than necessary interest rates.

John Maynard Keynes likened rentiers to usurers. He argued for lowering real interest rates as close as possible to zero to eliminate "rentier capital accumulation."[21] To guarantee the "euthanasia of the rentier," Keynes suggested that governments influence "two-thirds to three-fourths" of total investment.[22] Keynes had no doubt that "It is worse in an impoverished world to provoke unemployment than to disappoint the rentier."

Redefining Usury

"If your brother becomes poor, and cannot maintain himself with you; you shall maintain him, as a stranger and a sojourner he shall live with you. Take no interest from him or increase... You shall not lend him money at interest, nor give him your food for profit." (Leviticus 25:36-37)

Such injunctions are common in the Old Testament. For the times they made sense. In an agricultural society people borrow money to tide themselves over adversity. The crop has failed; the ox has died; or the barn burned down. Loans in such a society are for the relief of distress, and to profit from a neighbour's misfortune is clearly immoral. The church saw the logic of the law, and maintained the prohibition on interest, usury as it was called, throughout most of the Middle Ages.

But with the rise of commerce, especially in places like Northern Italy, the blanket prohibition of taking interest became harder to maintain. Commerce requires credit; it functions in a cash, not a subsistence environment. The rules designed for one kind of society did not fit the new one. Hence, in the thirteenth century, Thomas Aquinas distinguished between partnerships and simple loans. Someone who lent money to a merchant or a craftsman to finance a productive enterprise was entitled to a share in the profits. But Aquinas retained the prohibition of making money from loans used for consumption.

Even Aquinas' careful reasoning was made obsolete by the voyages of the late fifteenth century. In 1492 Columbus landed in the Bahamas; five years later Vasco da Gama reached India. The European conquest of other lands led to a flood of new money into Europe. Commerce, for years a specialty of Northern Italy, quickly became central to the Rhine valley in the very heart of Europe. The taking of interest became more and more common, but under all kinds of subterfuges.

It was John Calvin, the father of the Reformed and Presbyterian Churches, who finally called a spade a spade. In a letter to a friend, written in 1545, he reviewed all the arguments, biblical and philosophical, against the taking of interest and found them wanting. A loan at interest was legitimate provided it was profitable to both borrower and lender, was useful to the society as a whole, not just to the partners, and was at a rate of interest not exceeding the law of the land. In Geneva, where Calvin lived, the law of the land was five per cent. But, retaining the original intention of the biblical

Redefining Usury

(cont'd from previous page)

Law, Calvin insisted that loans to the poor must be interest free.

The form of Christian faith which Calvin laid out found its most enthusiastic response in the new commercial society which was growing up around trade in American silver and Asian spices. The most influential of Calvin's followers came from England, a country which hitherto had been somewhat of a backwater. But in the seventeenth century England replaced the Low Countries as the centre of European finance.

At the same time the English Calvinists, the Puritans, in alliance with the new commercial class managed to replace the Stuart monarchy, which pretended to be absolute, first with a republic, and finally with a constitutional monarchy under William of Orange. The drive behind the English revolution was a dislike of government interference in religious and commercial affairs. But in the process of disposing of a government whose interference they did not like, they undermined the notion of government interference of any kind.

The effect of this shift in thinking was to divorce political economy from ethics. The thinkers of the Middle Ages and the Reformation took for granted that society is an ethical entity and that the state should intervene in public affairs for the common good. But this outlook began to appear antiquated in the face of the new School of Political Arithmetic which drew its inspiration from the cool rationalism of Descartes, Bacon and Newton. They concluded that society should be understood, not as an organism, but as a machine, a machine which worked according to the interplay of impersonal forces.

If the economy, like the universe, is a machine, it has no ethics, it just works. In a world bewitched by Newtonian mechanics any ethical discussion of economics seemed bizarre. Only a lonely fringe of Christians insisted that the slave trade, one of the engines of British prosperity in the eighteenth century, was utterly immoral. It took a century for their case to be taken seriously. They won, finally, not because of the logic of their case, but because the trade had outlived its usefulness. In 1769 James Watt patented the steam engine; the Industrial Revolution was underway.

The Industrial Revolution was a change in human society comparable only to the shift from food gathering to agriculture. So vast was the transformation in Western society that the churches had to become vocal again. The Social Gospel movement was led by people like Walter

Redefining Usury

(cont'd from previous page)

Rauschenbusch in the U.S. and F.D. Maurice in England. Pope Leo XIII's celebrated encyclical, *Rerum Novarum*, published in 1891, marked the beginning of modern Catholic social teaching. These movements of the late nineteenth and early twentieth century concentrated on such questions as the social consequences of industry rather than commerce and finance.

Only in our time, especially after the U.S. created the debt crisis of the 1980s by driving nominal interest rates above 20% and real rates many times higher than their historical levels, have references to usury reappeared.

The similarities between the 1970s and the 1570s are intriguing. In our era floods of footloose money, chiefly Eurocurrencies, have destabilized world finance. In the sixteenth century a flood of silver into Europe plundered from the indigenous peoples of the Americas disrupted the financial order. Inflation followed in the sixteenth as in the twentieth century. But in the twentieth century governments responded to inflation with usurious interest rates and set off the era of speculative capitalism.

The loans made to less developed countries during the 1980s to refinance debts were no longer risk loans for investment in production. Nor were they distress loans to help the poor. Only the lenders stood to gain by insisting that overdue interest on Third World debt be repaid at the new higher rates. No one could argue that these loans were in the public interest. On the contrary, the austerity and structural adjustment conditions attached made the lives of the poorest sectors even more miserable.

In our era the original biblical injunction has been stood on its head. The prohibition of interest was to protect the poor from the money lenders. Now the poor are expected to protect the money lenders from any financial setback. Interest payments have become sacrosanct. No matter what else they have to cut--whether it be health care, education or social assistance--governments must meet their interest obligations. Principal payments can sometimes be postponed or rolled over into new loans and occasionally even forgiven as occurred under the Brady Plan. But the repayment of interest has become the one payment that must not be missed.

In searching for a new ethic for our day we should recall that the original thrust of the biblical injunction is to protect the poor from debt slavery.

THE WALL ST. CASINO

Back in 1936, John Maynard Keynes observed that, "when the capital development of a country becomes the by-product of the casino, the job is likely to be ill-done." Six decades later, these words apply more than ever to what is happening on Wall Street and Bay Street, with world-wide implications.

The world of finance became a global gambling casino through a combination of events. First, technological advances enabled financial markets to link together into a single computerized system, operating 24 hours a day. It costs only 18 cents to send a multi-million-dollar transaction across the ocean in a matter of seconds.

At the same time, mutual funds, pension funds and the so-called hedge funds (see glossary on following pages) became major investment vehicles.

As David Korten explains: "Today, when most people invest, very few buy shares in a company; instead they buy shares in these funds, which are run by fund managers who are evaluated on the basis of very short-term results. The obvious example is the mutual funds whose results are published on a daily basis. It increasingly turns out that what we have referred to as 'investment' is really a process of speculating, or betting, on very short-term price movements."[23]

The short time frames are very disruptive. They leave too little opportunity for investments to mature, and the kinds of return market players have come to expect exceed what most productive investments are able to yield. If a mutual fund does not keep up, it will find investors switching their money to other funds. Hence the pressure on fund managers to maintain high, short-term results is immense.

In the old industrial capitalism, the stock market played an important role. It was the place where companies raised capital to expand their production. A corporation wishing to open up a new plant would issue new stocks or bonds to finance its expansion. The stock market was seen as a mechanism for moving credit from savers to investors.

Dean Baker, Robert Poulin and Marc Schaberg show how stock and bond market trading now "has almost nothing to do with raising funds for investment. Players in the market now trade more than $100 worth of stocks and bonds for every dollar that non-financial corporations raise for new investment in plants and equipment. This ratio is almost four times what it was 30 years ago, and it keeps rising as innovative financiers develop ever more complex 'derivative' financial instruments, such as options, futures, and currency and equity swaps."[24]

These authors observe that, **over the U.S. business cycle that lasted from 1982 to 1990, not one new dollar had to be raised on Wall Street to finance investments in plant or equipment.** Corporations had saved enough themselves to finance all their new investments.

The following table illustrates how dramatically speculation has taken over U.S. stock and bond markets. For every dollar's worth of new stocks issued in the U.S. in 1992, $113.80 worth of stocks changed hands in speculative trades. Similarly, for every dollar raised through new issues of corporate bonds, $122.10 worth of existing bonds changed hands. Finally, for each new dollar the U.S. government borrowed from the market, $169.30 changed hands.

Table One
Speculative Trading Versus Productive Financing in the US
(figures are for 1992)

	Existing Stocks & Bonds Traded	New Stocks & Bonds Issued	Ratio of Trading of New Issues
Stock Market	$3.1 trillion	$26.8 billion	114 to 1
Corporate Bond Market	$8.2 trillion	$67.3 billion	122 to 1
US Government Securities Market	$44.4 trillion	$272.2 billion	169 to 1

Source: The Nation May 9, 1994 p.624

Another indication of the growing prominence of the financial sector is the increase in the volume of U.S. interest receipts on foreign loans compared to U.S. earnings on foreign direct investment (FDI). In the early 1960s, interest receipts were only about 20% as large as FDI earnings. At the beginning of the 1970s, the former were about 30% as large as the latter. By the beginning of the 1990s, interest receipts were about **40% larger** than FDI earnings.

A Glossary of Financial Terms

bonds - are like IOUs issued by governments or corporations. Bonds are an alternative to bank loans for borrowing money. Bonds are contracts purchased at a discount (that is below face value) on which the issuer is obliged to pay a specified amount (the par, face, or maturity value) at a certain date in the future (the maturity date). Most of the bonds discussed in this study are floating rate bonds whose interest rate or "yield" goes up and down in inverse relation to the price of the bond as it is bought and sold on the open market.

futures - a contract, traded on an organized exchange, to buy or sell a standardized amount of a product at a specific price on a future date. The same contract may be bought and sold several times before it comes due.

options - are similar to futures, except that instead of agreeing to actually exchange assets, the buyer purchases the option to exchange assets on a given future date if he or she wishes. Longer term options are called "warrants".

hedging - taking a position in a futures market opposite to that held or planned in a cash market. For example, a bakery that wants to avoid unexpected increases in the price of sugar might hedge by buying a contract for the future delivery of sugar at a predictable price.

speculation - buying or selling commodities, currencies, stocks, bonds or various derivatives in the hope of profiting from price fluctuations. Unlike hedgers, speculators take positions in futures markets without taking an offsetting position in cash markets.

derivatives - financial contracts whose value is based on, or derived from, the value of other contracts for tradable items such as commodities or currencies. For example, rather than gauging what might happen to an individual stock, the derivatives trader gambles that a whole stock market index will rise or fall.

hedge funds - private, unregulated investment funds that specialize in high risk, short term speculation on bonds, currencies, stock options and

A Glossary of Financial Terms

(cont'd from previous page)

derivatives. They require a minimum initial investment of US$1 million. Although these funds "hedge" their bets by diversifying their holdings among a number of markets, the term is actually a misnomer since these funds seldom hedge as defined above.

arbitraging - buying and selling bonds or currencies in one exchange for immediate resale or repurchase on another exchange to take advantage of small price differentials.

securities - tradable financial instruments such as bonds or stocks. Securitization is the pooling together of loans or assets for subsequent sale to investors.

swaps - agreements to purchase (or sell) a product on one date and to sell (or purchase) it back on a later date.

exchange rate - the price of one country's currency in another's currency; for example, on average during 1995 the Canadian dollar was worth 73 US cents.

eurocurrencies - deposits of dollars (Eurodollars) or other currencies (Euroyen or Euromarks or Eurofrancs etc.) outside the country issuing the currency. The name stems from the practice of depositing US dollars in Europe to avoid banking regulations, but the money could be held in Singapore or the Cayman Islands. Eurocurrency markets are markets where banks accept deposits and make loans in foreign currencies.

capital markets - markets in which financial instruments with maturities of more than one year are bought and sold.

money markets - markets in which financial instruments with maturities of less than one year, such as short-term Treasury bills, are bought and sold.

foreign direct investment - investments abroad in which the foreign investor is deemed to control the enterprise.

foreign portfolio investment - investments abroad in which the investor is deemed not to have a controlling interest such as ownership of minority shares in a company or government or corporate bonds.

In the early 1980s, at the height of the debt crisis before many loans were written down, interest receipts were more than twice as high as FDI earnings.

Furthermore, "the relative ascendancy of finance also shows up within FDI itself. The stock of U.S. FDI in the categories of banking, finance, insurance, and real estate has grown substantially faster than investment in other categories."[25] In the period 1970 to 1990, these finance categories rose from about 10% to around 30% of US FDI.

Interest Rate Futures

A prime example of the kind of change that has made financial markets more speculative is the invention in the late 1970s of futures contracts for interest rates. The premise for interest rate futures is that they allow corporations to hedge their future financial costs against unforeseen interest rate increases. Let's consider a simple example.

Suppose a company borrows $100 million at floating interest rates to build a factory. If the owners are worried that interest rates might rise, they can buy a swap contract for an imaginary $100 million loan. If interest rates do rise, the gains they make on the swap will cancel out the increased interest payments on the real loan. If rates fall, the losses on the swap cancel out the benefits derived from lower-than-anticipated borrowing costs. For a small fee, the company gains the security of knowing what its interest costs will be.

In order for this kind of hedging to take place, there have to be speculators willing to take a position in the market opposite to that of the hedging company. Under a sane financial system, companies would not have to worry as much about wild fluctuations, as exchange rates and interest rates would be more stable and predictable.

Although futures contracts on interest rates have only been around since the late 1970's, their total volume exceeds by a wide margin what might reasonably be needed by corporations wanting to hedge. It is currently estimated that the outstanding value of contracts on interest rate futures are worth more than half as much as the total U.S. Gross National

Product.[26] In April of 1995, the daily turnover in Canadian interest rate derivatives markets was worth US$15 billion.[27]

The Economist reports that the value of the total stock of derivatives contracts traded on exchanges or sold over the counter at the end of 1994 was US$20 trillion.[28] This is roughly equivalent to the estimated value of the world's total stock of productive fixed capital in 1993.

Derivatives are especially risky because they are usually purchased "on margin." Purchasing on margin means that the buyer makes only a small deposit worth a fraction of the total value of the contract. One of the causes of the 1929 stock market crash that ushered in the Great Depression was that too many stocks were bought on slim margins. When the market started to fall, purchasers could not afford to cover the full extent of their losses.

Today's situation may be even more precarious. As David Korten reports, "The largest [derivative] players may not be required to put up any money at all—even though their potential financial exposure may run into hundreds of millions of dollars."[29]

Hedge funds have a disproportionate effect on financial markets because they borrow additional money to leverage their bets. The most famous of these funds, George Soros's Quantum Fund, can borrow as much as 10 times the US$11 billion it directly controls. Thus Soros can have as much as US$110 billion at play in the financial markets at any one time. The borrowing the hedge funds do ties up money that could be more productively used to build houses and factories or plant crops.[30]

Huge Profits, Huge Losses

All of this buying and selling can potentially reap huge profits for the financiers. Of course, it can also lead to huge losses. A single derivatives trader, Nick Leeson, caused the bankruptcy of Britain's Barings Bank by running up nearly US$1.2 billion in losses on derivatives trading in the Asian market. Copper trader Yasuo Hamanaka, working for Japan's Sumitomo Corporation, racked up an estimated US$2.6 billion worth of losses over the past ten years.[31] A trader for Daiwa Bank, also of Japan, lost $1.5 billion over 11 years on the New York bond market.[32]

What does all this activity really accomplish? Defenders of the system will say that it allows companies involved in producing real goods and services to stabilize their finances through hedging. In theory, by using the futures market, a company can know exactly what its raw material or financial costs will be.

The ability of a company to hedge depends on the willingness of a speculator to take an opposite position in the futures market. In practice, there is substantially more speculation than hedging going on. A survey of 530 U.S. non-financial corporations found that 75% of the respondents use derivatives to hedge their financial exposures, which is not unexpected. What is surprising is that 40% of the companies surveyed are also speculating on derivatives.[33] Significantly, these are all non-financial corporations. Speculation is by no means confined to financial companies and the hedge funds.

While banks, insurance companies, investment firms and hedge funds are the chief architects of the speculative economy, they are not the only players. We cannot assume that all corporations or all investment portfolios fall neatly into categories labeled "financial" or "industrial" capital. For example, British Petroleum's director of money transactions has stated that "Our currency dealing is at least as important as our oil trading."

General Motors Acceptance, which finances purchases of GM cars, is one of the largest financial institutions in the United States. In 1993, "General Motors and General Electric both made more profits from their internal financial subsidiaries ... than they did manufacturing real automotive or electronic products."[34]

As finance grows to dominate industrial capital, investors rely less and less on a paid labour force either to produce or purchase the products they trade. They pay less heed to Henry Ford's admonition that factory owners must pay workers enough to enable them to buy the products they manufacture. In contrast to his company's founder, the current chairman of Ford brazenly told the World Economic Forum that his company wants to employ low-wage but "supercompetitive labor forces that will raise productivity and quality of manufactures... to world class levels".[35]

In 1995, Ford paid its Mexican assembly line workers between

US$0.79 and US$1.26 an hour at its Cuautitlan plant near Mexico City. Skilled trade workers received between US$1.43 to US$1.64 an hour.[36] At the same time, the average hourly wage (excluding overtime) paid in the Canadian auto industry was $24.59 an hour.[37] At the prevailing exchange rate, this was equivalent to US$17.96, or 17 times as much as a low-skilled Mexican assembly worker and 11 times as much for skilled trades.

Advocates of globalized production will say that the Mexican workers are paid less because they are less productive. However, a study of the Ford automobile engine plant in Hermosillo found that the Mexican plant had achieved 80% of the machine efficiency and 75% of the labour productivity of a comparable U.S. facility. Meanwhile, Mexican workers were paid less than one-tenth of their U.S. counterparts.[38]

Growth of Pension and Mutual Funds

In recent years, investment patterns in the U.S. and Canada have changed dramatically. One of the most important developments is the growth of pension funds and mutual funds. Many working people with modest incomes are members of pension plans where retirement savings are withheld from their pay by their employers. These deferred wages are invested on the stock and bond markets by pension fund managers.

U.S. pension funds with some US$4 trillion worth of assets are mostly managed by the trust departments of the giant "money centre" banks. These pension funds alone hold about one-third of U.S. corporate shares and two-fifths of corporate bonds.[39]

In Canada, pension fund administrators manage about $360 billion worth of workers' savings.[40] Many people also have Registered Retirement Savings Plans (RRSPs) invested in mutual funds. Mutual funds are arrangements that pool many small investors' money to buy a variety of financial instruments such as stocks and bonds. Some mutual funds are known as "income funds" that aim to earn steady returns. Others, known as "growth funds," make riskier investments aiming for high yields. Canadian mutual funds now control about $146 billion worth of assets, up from $5 billion in 1982.[41]

In the United States, mutual funds have just overtaken pension funds as the most important players on the stock exchanges. During the first three months of 1996, mutual funds bought US$61 billion worth of stocks in the U.S.[42] Mutual funds can undertake riskier ventures than pension funds, which are confined by law to "investment grade" instruments.

Mutual funds have taken over the financing role of the largest banks in the so-called "emerging markets" of Asia and Latin America. Almost two-thirds of the foreign investment in Latin America between 1993 and mid-1995 came from mutual funds.

Business Week describes how a new class of investment fund managers commands international financial markets: "Increasingly dominated by American mutual- and hedge-fund investors controlling perhaps US$2 trillion in assets, this investor class is far different from the patient banks and multilateral development agencies that once provided the globe's international capital supply."[43] This set of hot money managers can move investments from U.S. Treasury bills to Mexican stocks to German government bond options just by picking up the telephone.

Unfortunately, working people have little say in where their pension money gets invested. Ed Finn gives the example of the Ontario Municipal Employees' Retirement Fund which invested in the MDS Health Group Ltd. MDS operates a chain of private medical laboratories. As Finn notes: "This investment not only contradicts the union's policy opposing private health care, but actually takes jobs away from unionized workers."[44]

Finn notes that pension money is used to cover the cost of moving plants from Canada to low-wage areas such as Mexico. The employees, who actually own the pension money, end up financing the loss of their own jobs because all the decision-making power is vested with the pension fund managers.

Speculation Distorts Priorities

Speculative capitalism distorts economic and social life as investors seek short-term gains rather than engage in long-term productive investments. An example of the perverse behavior of speculative markets is the sell-off that periodically occurs on Wall Street following reports of a stronger than expected growth in U.S. employment. Instead of welcoming the news as a sign that there would be more paying customers to buy their products, investors sell their stocks and bonds.

The perverse logic driving this behaviour is the fear that strong employment growth might spark renewed inflation or lead to higher wages and a more militant workforce, even in the absence of inflation. Financiers dread inflation because it cuts into the returns they earn on their investments.

As James Laxer explains, "What bond-holders care about is the rate of return on capital. They have a morbid fear of inflation since loans repaid in inflated currency aren't worth as much as those repaid in stable currency."[45] The bond-holders also relish the higher profits they make when real interest rates are kept high by central bankers' adherence to tight monetary policies.

THE POWER OF FINANCIAL MARKETS

Prime Minister Chrétien is far from the only person to observe how dependence on global finance has put into question the sovereignty of the nation state. Many other voices declare that financial markets have become more powerful than national governments in determining monetary and exchange rate policies. The idea of the withering away of state power is propagated by the business media, claimed by the investor class itself, echoed by some academic economists, and re-reinforced by central bankers and Finance Ministers who say their hands are tied by the financial markets.

The news media have popularized the notion of the powerless state. For example, Business Week (March 20, 1995:48) reports that some observers say the managers of "hot money" have become "a sort of shadow world government— one that is irretrievably eroding the concept of the sovereign powers of a nation state".[46] Business Week then cites a New York banker who says, "Countries don't control their own destiny. If they don't discipline themselves, the world market will do it for them."

Major players in the financial markets do not hesitate to make extravagant claims about their power. Listen, for example, to Walter Wriston, former chair of Citicorp, one of the largest U.S. financial corporations. Wriston boasts about the power wielded by "200,000 monitors in trading rooms all over the world [who conduct] a kind of global plebiscite on the monetary and fiscal policies of governments issuing currencies."[47]

Wriston recalls what happened after François Mitterrand became President of France: "The market took one look at his policies and within six months the capital flight forced him to reverse course."

Some academic economists echo the same message. Rudy Dornbusch of MIT asserts: "The global capital markets will punish any country falling from the path of reform. [The unforgiving foreign exchange and global bond markets] are the world's disciplinarians [forcing] countries to embrace austerity."[48]

Critics from the left of the political spectrum seem to agree. Gary Teeple writes that "The rise of foreign currency and international capital markets... meant not only that these functions were increasingly outside the control of national regulation, but also that they increasingly set the limits, as independent markets, on national policies with respect to credit systems, money supply, exchange and interest rates, debt-management, investment policies, and taxation."[49]

If one concedes that financial markets largely rule the world, then all that is left for governments and central banks is to try to please these markets by pursuing the policies the bond traders demand: low inflation enforced through monetarist policies of high real interest rates and high unemployment, and policies of fiscal austerity. Ultimately, this represents an abdication of power to wealthy investors and their interests. It means that governments must give up any pretense of truly working for the common good. In essence, this means abandoning the most basic principles of democracy.

This is the position adopted by the Canadian government. Prime Minister Chrétien argues that the government can retain sovereignty only as long as it pursues policies of fiscal austerity. He says, "It is true that putting our house in order does limit what a government can do in the short run. But it does not mean we are surrendering sovereignty to the markets. In fact, ***the more solid our fiscal shape, the less vulnerable*** we are to the whims of those young traders in red suspenders."[50]

Subservience to the demands of global bond traders can also be discerned in the speeches and actions of Canada's central bank governor and the Minister of Finance. The Governor of the Bank of Canada, Gordon Thiessen, argues that the leverage he has in financial markets is very small. He maintains that the Bank of Canada can only control very short-term interest rates and can only affect longer-term rates by reassuring the financial markets that it will not let up on its fight against inflation. Thiessen also says that the Minister of Finance must keep spending in check.

Finance Minister Paul Martin reiterated this position in his 1996 budget: "The best way to reduce interest rates is to continue to keep inflation low and get government deficits and debts under control."[51]

Currency Trading

There is no doubt that the raw market power of the private currency traders can overwhelm the resources available to central banks for intervention in foreign exchange markets. The Economist observes that the **total** foreign currency reserves of all the industrialized countries' governments amount to about US$640 billion.[52] Meanwhile, the **daily** turnover on international money markets is twice as large: US$1.3 trillion. Furthermore, the central banks would never throw all their reserves into the market.

Allen Metzler estimates that if all the world's central banks tried to act together to protect a currency from a speculative attack, the most they could muster would be US$14 billion a day. For every dollar the central banks could marshal, the private markets have 93. Therefore, the central banks can be outbid **if** speculators have the resolve to do so.

The recent historical record shows that, **when speculators make a determined effort**, they can overwhelm government attempts to defend a given exchange rate. The best known example is what happened to the British pound in 1992. George Soros "sold US$10 billion worth of British pounds in a bet against the success of British Prime Minister John Major's effort to maintain the pound's value. In doing so, he was credited with a major role in forcing a devaluation of the pound that contributed to breaking up the system of fixed exchange rates that governments were trying to put into place in the European Union.

"Fixed exchange rates are anathema for speculators because they eliminate the volatility on which speculators depend. For his role in protecting the opportunity for speculative profits, Soros extracted an estimated US$1 billion from the financial system for his investment funds."[53]

However, it is important to realize that concerted attacks on an individual currency, like Soros' against the pound, are rare. In normal daily trading, the actions of speculators who sell a currency are mostly offset by other traders who want to buy at a fractionally lower or higher price. There is still some room for central banks, especially if they act together in a co-ordinated fashion, to intervene successfully. For instance, in 1995 the U.S. and Japanese central banks successfully co-ordinated efforts to raise the value of the dollar against the yen.

Nevertheless, there is no doubt that the ability of central banks to influence exchange rates is limited in this era of speculative capitalism. Currently, the Bank of Canada only intervenes in currency markets to maintain "orderly market conditions in the context of a floating exchange rate".[54] The Bank will try to smooth out "sharp short-run movements in the dollar," but does not pretend to try to support it at any given level through open market trading. The Bank's chief influence on the value of the Canadian dollar is its preference for high real interest rates. These attract investment into bonds denominated in Canadian dollars and thereby support the exchange value of the loonie.

The Bond Market

James Laxer calls the bond market "the most powerful force in contemporary capitalism."[55] The power of the bond market stems from the direct influence it has on government finances and on interest rates. When floating rate bonds are bought and sold on the open market, both their price and their yield (that is, the interest rate they pay) fluctuate. The interest rate paid always moves in the opposite direction to the price of the bond.

Thus, if enough bond-holders want to sell a certain kind of bond—say, a government's 90-day Treasury bills—and buyers will only purchase them if the price is discounted, the effect is to push up the interest rate for new issues of those bonds. Since the financial markets are all linked together, there will be upward pressure on all that country's interest rates.

Bond trading can be more complicated than the buying and selling of currencies. Speculators on the bond markets take into account many factors when deciding when to buy, sell or hold their positions. First, there is the risk factor. Buyers have to decide whether the issuer will be able to make all interest payments when due and redeem the bonds for their full face value when they reach maturity. The higher the risk, the higher the interest rate they will demand.

Furthermore, speculators contemplating selling one country's bonds and buying another's to take advantage of higher interest rates in the second country must take into account not only the political risks but also the risk of changes in the exchange rate between the two countries' currencies during the period they hold the bonds.

As with the normal currency market described above, in a normal bond market there will always be willing buyers to purchase whatever bonds sellers wish to dispose of at slightly higher or lower prices. In fact, a price margin of only 3 to 10 cents per $100 of a bond's face value (0.03% to 0.1%) is enough to entice institutional investors to make profitable trades on the Canadian bond market today.

In the early 1980s, the difference between buying and selling prices was between 10 and 25 cents per $100 (0.1% to 0.25% of face value). Even though these price margins are very small, they are still large enough for speculators to make substantial profits as they trade in thousands or millions of dollars' worth of bonds at a time.

Only under exceptional circumstances will issuers have to discount prices by large amounts before they can find willing buyers. For instance, during the first month of Mexico's 1994-95 peso crisis, some of its bonds fell by over 20%. In mid-January of 1995, when the Clinton Administration was trying to persuade a reluctant Congress to approve a bail-out for Mexico, the Mexican government was having trouble selling new issues of its bonds. In order to entice buyers back into the market, Mexico was reportedly "willing to give virtually whatever interest rate investors demanded to make sure that all its bonds were taken."[56]

Those three-month bonds were sold with interest rates of 19.75%. On the same day, 90-day U.S. dollar bonds paying 6% interest were available on the New York market. Investors in Mexican bonds enjoyed a risk premium of 13.75% and in the end faced little risk since Clinton used his executive powers to establish a bail-out fund without a Congressional vote.

The distinction between extraordinary conditions, like the peso crisis, and normal market conditions is very important. As we shall see in the next chapter, there is ample scope for the Bank of Canada to take a more active role in the bond markets. In Chapter Four we shall delve more deeply into the dynamics of the Mexican crisis. There we shall see the double standard of the bond traders. They want free rein, unencumbered by government regulation, to make high profits from risky loans to "emerging markets" like Mexico. But, when these countries' economies become seriously distorted by all the speculation, the global investors also want governments to bail them out, as the Clinton Administration did with its rescue package for Mexico's investors.

Monetary Policy

The influence of the money markets on monetary policy is a daily reality. If bond traders dislike a central bank's efforts to lower interest rates because they fear a bout of inflation, they may counteract it by selling off that country's bonds and driving up its interest rates. If interest rates rise too high, they will discourage borrowing for productive investments or purchases of homes, appliances and other big-ticket items. The effect will be higher unemployment and higher debt servicing costs for governments.

The threat of capital flight is a powerful weapon in the hands of the bond traders. This new investor class is unlike the patient investors of an earlier era who bought and held onto government bonds because they were secure, albeit low-yielding investments. Today's bond-holders are willing to quickly take their money out of a country's bonds in search of higher returns elsewhere if a central bank tries to lower interest rates faster than other jurisdictions, or if the bond traders fear their returns will be eroded by inflation.

Are central banks totally powerless? Ironically, one of the most enthusiastic cheerleaders for the demise of state power—the conservative British magazine _The Economist_—argues that central banks are not really that weak. In a special survey of the world economy, the magazine's editors generally applaud the loss of government regulatory power to the financial markets. Nevertheless, they argue that the loss of sovereignty is not so complete. _The Economist_ asserts that "the fears about governments being left powerless to defend their countries' economic interests have been overdone."[57]

The magazine's editors maintain that, if governments are willing to accept floating exchange rates, they can still have an independent monetary policy. Although central banks have less ability to intervene in open markets where their trading is dwarfed by private transactions, they can still set short-term interest rates by more direct means. For example, the Bank of Canada can set the "overnight rate" charged on loans that private banks make to each other to clear accounts at the end of each business day.

The Economist says central banks can still set reserve requirements for private banks and determine the interest rate that will be charged on those reserves: "So long as banks need reserves and so long as central banks keep their monopoly [as supplier of reserves], they will retain their control over short-term rates."[58]

This argument remains true for the United States. However, in Canada the situation is complicated by the Mulroney government's 1991 decision to discontinue reserve requirements for Canadian banks. In the next chapter we shall see how the Bank of Canada has largely backed away from intervention in the bond markets. In Canada's case, the central bank's weakness is largely a self-inflicted wound. However, as we shall see, it need not be so powerless.

From Speculation to Sustenance

Confronting the growth of the speculative economy requires insight, creativity, and concerted action. First and foremost, however, it requires the will and the desire to change the course of economics. This will is not evident in the behaviour of most governments. As individuals, we too, must decide where we stand.

Ultimately, economics is about choices and values. We can choose to let speculative capitalism continue in its advance. If we have money invested, even if it is only a small amount in a Registered Retirement Savings Plan, we may stand to gain in the short term. But at what cost to the vast majority of the world's inhabitants? What kind of world will be left for future generations? Will our planet's very ability to sustain life be undermined to enrich a few in the short term?

As Manfred Bienefeld points out, the paradox of the exploitative economic system we live in "may have been best summarized by a western Canadian farmer describing his desperate efforts to stave off foreclosure by his creditors. While setting out his plans for planting, weeding and spraying, he suddenly pauses to say: 'Of course I'm destroying the soil, but it's my only hope of survival.'"[59]

The same process is going on at a global level. Among the poorer nations of the South, human beings and ecosystems are being savagely exploited to finance payments for external debt. Doors are being flung wide-open to corporate exploitation. In the North, too, we are subject to a similar process, being told that national debts accumulated due to high interest payments and tax breaks to the wealthy must now be paid for through cuts to social programs. Meanwhile, to remain "competitive" in the global race to the bottom, we are encouraged to deregulate corporate activities, even if this means lower wages and greater ecological destruction.

It is possible to imagine an alternative. To some, this may seem to be utopian. Yet, the world economy as it functions today is obviously far from sane. At the very least, we can think of the values we would like to embody in an economics of the future. We need a vision to guide us if we are to confront the forces of speculative finance.

As we have already seen, the root meaning of the word economy (or "oikonomia") is the care and management of our home, which begins in our community and ultimately stretches to include the Earth itself. Economics need not mean accumulating wealth for the few at the cost of the many. It can be about finding ways to manage our common household so that the quality of life is sustained and ultimately enhanced for all. Ultimately, then, economics must move from a quest for short-term gain to the art of long-term sustenance.

CHAPTER THREE

Canada Caught in the Currents

Canada is very vulnerable to the currents of speculative capitalism. *The Globe and Mail* reports that "The growth of continental trade and the harmonization of Canadian and U.S. securities regulations means Canada's capital market has virtually fused with that of the United States. Canadian companies issued 66% of their bonds and 17% of their equity [in 1995] in the United States."[60]

One fallout of the loss of control over our own financial market is the degree to which federal and provincial politicians bow to pressure from financiers to "restructure" social programs. As governments adopt the monetary and fiscal policies described in Chapter Two, they continue to ignore employment creation and to undermine our social safety net.

Over the past decade, our social programs have not just been eroded; their very existence has been challenged. We have witnessed attacks on social assistance, unemployment insurance, public pensions, funding for post-secondary education, and even Canada's health care system.

Governments are reducing their commitment to employment creation. They are also reducing their role in the administration of public programs. The processes of privatization and decentralization that are going on in Canada correspond to the demands of the financial markets.

The push from the right to continue in this direction is getting stronger. At the August 1996 meeting of premiers and territorial leaders, Premiers Ralph Klein and Mike Harris attempted to persuade the other leaders to endorse their goal of complete decentralization of Canada's social programs. They had to back down in the face of opposition from the premiers of the poorer provinces. However, they were successful in keeping the door open on the discussion about Medicare.

If Klein gets his way, Ottawa would have no ability to levy cash penalties against provinces not complying with "national standards" for Medicare—effectively opening the door to a two-tiered health care system. The decentralization of social programs sought by Klein and Harris would be the undoing of any gains made in narrowing regional disparities in the country.

Our society has already become a meaner place for the poor, especially, though not only, in the wealthier provinces. Snitch lines for reporting against people on social assistance and programs like workfare—compulsory work for welfare schemes—are just two examples of what governments in provinces such as Ontario, British Columbia, Alberta and New Brunswick are getting away with.

The "deregulation" of provincial services permitted by the Canada Health and Social Transfer (CHST) is resulting in real horror stories. Alarming numbers of individuals and families are falling between the cracks of provincial social assistance regulations. Growing numbers of unemployed people are travelling the country looking for work—people for whom no government takes responsibility. End Legislated Poverty in Vancouver, Low Income Families Together in Toronto, and the National Anti-Poverty Organization in Ottawa are just three of the anti-poverty groups that are doing an excellent job of documenting these stories.

At the same time that poor people are becoming peripheral in this country, the economy is working well for the banks and for the investors who dictate government fiscal and social policy. Canada's six largest banks had record profits of $5.2 billion in 1995, while rates of unemployment and underemployment, especially for the young and for women, continue to be unacceptably high. The unemployed receive lower benefits.

As this study is being written late in 1996, only 42% of the unemployed are eligible for any benefits at all. Before the Free Trade Agreement was implemented, 87% of jobless Canadians received Unemployment Insurance. Despite promises by the financiers that some short-term pain would lead to prosperity, there are no signs of improvement for the working and middle classes.

Portfolio Debt Growing

One measure of our growing vulnerability is our foreign debt. Our net foreign debt (including all government and private loans and equity investments) grew to $339 billion at the end of 1995, three times as large as it was in 1980 when speculative capitalism began to assert itself. The composition of our international liabilities has also changed in recent years. So has the way in which the federal government finances its debts.

From 1952 through 1976, most non-resident investment in Canada was foreign direct investment, or FDI as it is called. Non-resident investments are classified as FDI when the foreign owner is deemed to control an enterprise. Direct investors have more of a stake in maintaining a viable local market for their products over the long haul. When they establish factories, retail outlets or other services in a country, direct investors expect to recover their costs and earn profits over a number of years.

Since 1977, portfolio investment has become more significant than foreign direct investment. Foreign portfolio investment includes non-resident purchases of shares in companies based in Canada (where the purchaser is not deemed to hold a controlling interest) and offshore holdings of corporate and government bonds.

In contrast to FDI, portfolio investment is more volatile. Minority stock holdings or bonds can quickly be sold and the proceeds reinvested in another country where short-term returns are higher.

Chart Three shows how foreign portfolio investment overtook FDI in the late 1970s and has grown much more quickly over the last 15 years. Chart Four shows the distribution of Canada's foreign liabilities. Provincial governments and their utilities owe 25% of this debt. The fastest growth in recent years has been in borrowing by provincial governments.[61]

Chart Three
Direct and Portfolio Foreign Investment in Canada
C$ billions 1970 - 1995

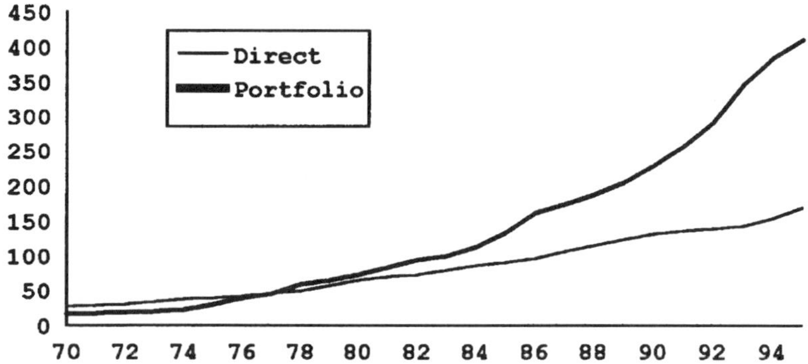

Source: Statistics Canada: 67-202 Table 1

National Debt More Problematic Now

Chart Four
Distribution Of Canada's Foreign Liabilities
percentages - end of 1995

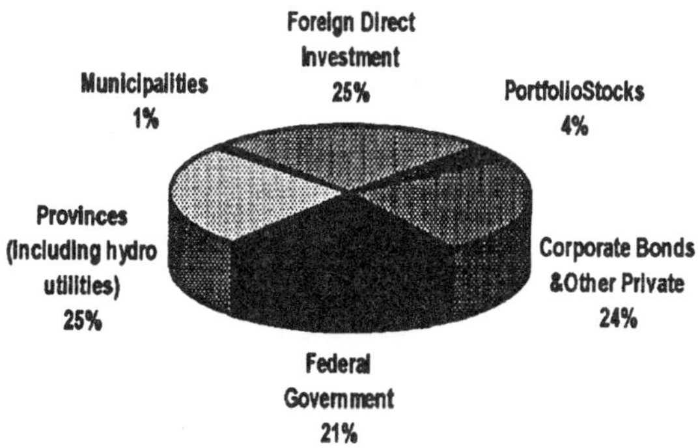

Source: Statistics Canada 67-202

In the past, we in ECEJ argued that the national debt—that is, the money owed by the federal government—was not as problematic as our foreign debt, since it was owed mostly to Canadians. In fact, government debt instruments were regarded by many as secure assets. Generations of Canadians of modest means bought Canada Savings Bonds and held them until maturity.

Private banks still anchor their investment portfolios with secure government debt. As long as the average real interest rate paid on government debt was only 0.9%, as it was from 1962 through 1981, the cost of servicing the debt was manageable. Since most of the debt was held in Canada, we could always say we owed it to "ourselves," although the payments accrued disproportionately to the wealthy. Nevertheless, most of these interest payments recirculated within the domestic economy.

What turned the national debt from an asset into a problem? Two factors are most important.

First, the cost of servicing the debt grew as real interest rates rose across the board after 1981. The rise in Canadian rates that year followed a world-wide trend towards higher rates that started in the United States. After the U.S. raised its rates above 20% in 1981 to fight inflation and stem an attack on the U.S. dollar, Canada followed suit. The Canadian prime rate peaked at 22.5% in 1981.

Chart Five
Average Real Interest Rates Paid on Public Debts 1962-1995

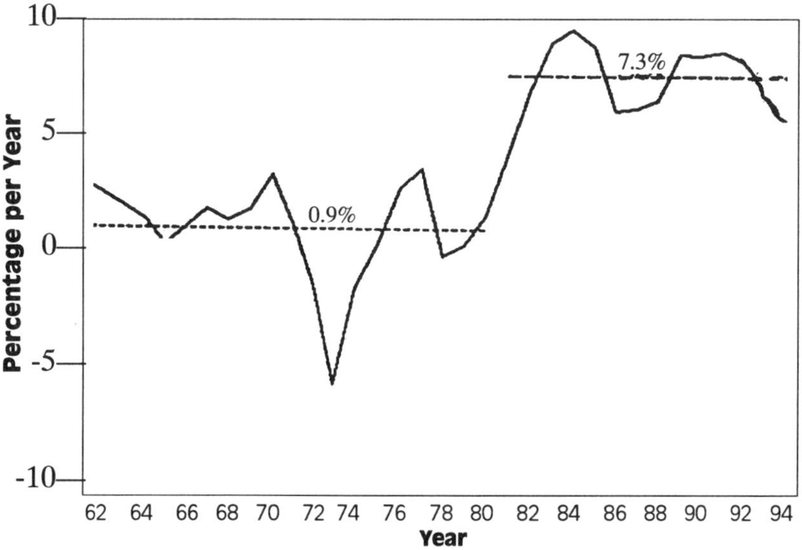

Source: Osberg and Fortin (1996) Unnecessary Debts p.33, and Department of Finance.

Chart Six
Canada's Net Foreign Debt and Federal Debt Owed Abroad
C$ billions 1985-1995

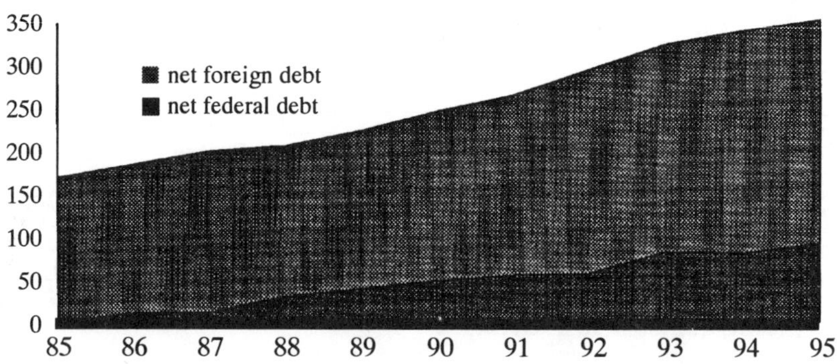

Although nominal rates soon fell back, along with the rate of inflation, real interest rates have remained high for the last 15 years. As Chart Five shows, the average real interest rate paid on public debt grew to 7.3% over the years 1982-1995, more than eight times as much as it had been from 1962 to 1981.

Secondly, as Charts Six and Eight show, the portion of the federal debt owed abroad grew rapidly after 1983. Meanwhile, a smaller share of federal debt was held by the Bank of Canada and in Canada Savings Bonds.

As the distribution of government debt changed and real interest rates rose, payments on the national debt increasingly became transfers from taxpayers of modest means to wealthy bond-holders, many of whom reside abroad. Canada's national debt became a more serious problem after it became caught in the currents of speculative capitalism. While more of the debt is held abroad, it is also true that wealthy Canadians are also prone to dump Canadian bonds unless they receive high returns and protection against inflation.

Chart Six shows how borrowing by the federal government accounted for more and more of our external debt over the years 1985-1995. In fact, almost one-half of the increase in Canada's net foreign debt over the period was due to federal borrowing abroad.

Bond-holders Flex Their Muscles

As the new class of investors—both foreign and domestic—described in the last chapter come to hold more of Canada's public debt, they assert their political and financial power. Business people seldom miss an opportunity to remind us of the government's weakness in the face of global capital. As Thomas Kierans, president of the C.D. Howe Institute, put it: "We're losing our sovereignty... We are prisoners to the international financial markets."[62]

In their public discourse, the financial elite constantly warn us about the dangers of the federal government's annual deficits and accumulated debt. They also frequently warn about the dangers of renewed inflation, sometimes invoking the image of poor widows on fixed incomes who cannot afford to have their pensions eroded by rising prices.

The policy proposals that the investor class advocates to fight deficits and inflation are very explicit. They want the government to fight the deficit by cutting its spending, including spending on social programs. They want the Bank of Canada to pursue a tight money policy that fights inflation through high real interest rates and high unemployment, regardless of the human cost. They warn that, if Canadian interest rates fall too far below rates in other countries, there will be an outflow of capital and a run on the Canadian dollar.

However, Canadian experience over the latter half of 1995 and the first three-quarters of 1996 contradicts these predictions. The fact is that the Bank of Canada successfully cut its benchmark overnight interest rate 17 times over 17 months. The overnight loan rate, also known as "the bank rate", fell from 7.64% in June of 1995 to 4% in early October of 1996. In response, the private Canadian banks lowered their prime lending rate to 5.5%, 2.75 percentage points lower than the 8.25% prime rate in the U.S.

All this occurred without major capital flight or downward pressure on the Canadian dollar. A principal reason why there was no large outflow of capital from Canada was because investors recognized that the Canadian economy had been so flattened by high unemployment and the effects of government spending cuts that they perceived no danger of renewed inflation. Furthermore, higher inflation in the U.S. than in Canada deterred investors from moving their money there.

Hypocrisy

The investors' warnings about the perils of government debt involve a massive amount of hypocrisy. These financiers do not **really** want the national debt paid off. Rather, they want to go on profiting from their holdings of government bonds. Their warnings about inflation have little to do with the plight of poor widows on fixed incomes. What they are worried about is the lost profits that would result if real interest rates were to come down through even a modest increase in prices.

Far from caring about pensioners, their prescription for cutting public pension plans and privatizing retirement savings amounts to a scheme for enlarging the amount of capital at play in private markets.

We must be careful not to concede too much power to the myths that the money market managers themselves propagate. The more they can convince us that we are powerless in the face of such anonymous forces as the global capital market, the more influence they have over public policy.

Instead of caving in to the financiers' demands for further spending cuts and high interest rates, we must be prepared to counter their arguments with solid, factual information about the real causes of government debts. To understand the room for manoeuvre that does exist, we need to appreciate why the federal debt grew as it did.

How the Federal Debt Grew

Several different studies, using distinct methodologies, have probed into the actual causes of Canadian government debts and deficits. Each of these studies employed a unique methodology, measuring different but related phenomena over diverse time frames. Our purpose here is not to evaluate each of these studies or to come up with a definitive explanation. Rather, we intend to show how several studies support one basic conclusion: that the federal debt was **not** caused by excessive spending, least of all on social transfers to people in need.

In *Shooting the Hippo*, Linda McQuaig describes how Hideo Mimoto, chief of the social security section of Statistics Canada, produced what is perhaps the most comprehensive study of the causes of Canadian government debts and deficits. Yet Mimoto's original work was never officially released, despite the fact that his initial study had been vetted and approved by the senior researcher at the Canadian Tax Foundation and by economists with both the Department of Finance and the Economic Council of Canada.

Due to the politically explosive nature of his findings, Mimoto had to rewrite his original study before it appeared in the June 1991 edition of *Canadian Economic Observer*. Nevertheless, the published version that appeared in Statistics Canada's own scholarly journal clearly showed that fiscal and monetary policies, not social spending, caused Canadian government debt to grow.

McQuaig describes the political furore that followed when officials in the Department of Finance objected to the publication of a study that contradicted the political position of the Mulroney government regarding the need for spending cuts. Statistics Canada then took the extraordinary step of disassociating itself from its own study by publishing a disclaimer in a subsequent (August 1991) issue of the *Canadian Economic Observer.*

Mimoto's original study, dated June 27, 1990, concluded that 50% of the increase in federal debt between 1975 and 1989 was due to a relative drop in tax revenues, and 44% was caused by soaring interest rates. Only 6% of the growth in the debt could be attributed to program spending. And only one-third of that spending increment was dedicated to social programs. Unlike other studies, Mimoto evaluates the impact of changes in taxation policy, as well as changes in interest costs and government spending.

Table Two summarizes research by W. Irwin Gillespie, which complements Mimoto's findings. Gillespie maintains that the federal debt snowball initially started to roll in the 1970s because of revenue losses due to tax policy changes. The Liberal Finance Ministers of the Trudeau era introduced various changes to corporate income taxes, personal income taxes, and the manufacturers' sales tax which are summarized in the accompanying table.

As the table shows, the main beneficiaries of these tax changes were corporations, individual investors with interest and dividend income, and people wealthy enough to save money in private Registered Retirement Savings Plans. It is also noteworthy that some of these tax measures assisted the buildup of pools of speculative capital such as the mutual funds that thrive on tax-sheltered RRSPs.

Table Two
The Tax Breaks That Started the Debt Ball Rolling

	Finance Minister	Policy Change
A. Reductions in the effective corporate income tax rate		
1972	John Turner	corporate tax rate reduced to 40%; machinery depreciated over 2 years
1975	John Turner	5% tax credit for investments in buildings, machinery & equipment
1977	Donald MacDonald	extended duration and rates of investment tax credit for depressed regions
1978	Jean Chrétien	increased basic and regional investment tax credits and made them permanent
B. Personal income tax expenditures		
1971	Edgar Benson	increased allowable deductions for pension plans and Registered Retirement Savings Plans (RRSPs)
	John Turner	increased personal and elderly exemptions; deductions for post-secondary students, interest and dividend income, home ownership savings and pension income
	Donald MacDonald	increased allowable deductions for pension plans and RRSPs and employment expenses; raised limits on dividend tax credit, the personal credit and capital losses
	Jean Chrétien	introduced deductions on registered retirement investment funds; increased deduction for employment expenses
C. Reductions in rate for the Manufacturers Sales Tax		
1974	John Turner	reduced tax rate on building and construction materials from 12% to 5%
1978	Jean Chrétien	reduced rate on other manufactured goods from 12% to 9%

Source: Adapted from W. Irwin Gillespie in Osberg and Fortin (1996) ***Unnecessary Debts*** p.15-18.

Other studies of the origins of the debt yield different results because they use different methodologies and cover more recent time periods. These studies put less emphasis on changes in taxation and concentrate instead on the effects of high interest rates.

A study by the Dominion Bond Rating Service (DBRS) looks at why the debt grew over the fiscal years 1984 through 1994. Unlike Mimoto, the DBRS does not look at changes in taxation policy over the period. The DBRS concludes that "Of the total debt outstanding at March 31, 1994, the program spending imbalance accounted for a modest 16% or $82 billion of the $508 billion net debt. The remaining 84% of the debt is due to compounding interest on the relatively modest program expenditure deficiency."[63]

A recent book entitled *Unnecessary Debts,* edited by Lars Osberg and Pierre Fortin, provides further evidence that social spending did not cause Canadian government debts. Fortin looks in particular at the effects of the macroeconomic policies of the Bank of Canada and the federal government that resulted in the two recessions beginning in 1982 and 1990. He concludes that "The difference between program spending and tax revenues is only marginally responsible for the debt explosion since 1981, while the mediocre macroeconomic performance explains 60% of it... The remainder of the debt (40%) is attributable to a greater difference between the average interest rate on the debt and the growth rate of GDP."[64]

In the same volume, Michael McCracken of Informetrica takes a different approach. He uses an econometric forecasting model to calculate what would have happened if the Bank of Canada had followed a policy of keeping Canadian interest rates in line with those in the United States between 1989 and 1995. He finds that the result would have been faster economic growth and much lower unemployment. "In addition, Canada's debt burden would have fallen slightly instead of rising substantially."[65]

Finally, in a background paper prepared for the 1996 Alternative Federal Budget, Canadian Auto Workers economist Jim Stanford estimates that "the *combination* of higher interest rates and slower growth *directly* caused 83% of the post-1981 growth of the debt-to-GDP ratio, and 112% of the rise in this ratio since 1990. At the interest and growth rates that prevailed from 1950 to 1980, Canada's debt burden would have been declining since 1986, and would equal just over 30% today (rather than approximately 72% at present). These estimates are extremely conservative, in that they do not consider the *indirect* beneficial effects of lower interest rates and stronger economic growth on the federal government's operating balance."[66]

While one might quibble with the methodologies used in any one of these studies, taken together they overwhelmingly point to one conclusion: **Canadian government debts are chiefly caused by the very policies that the investor class advocates—especially high interest rates—and not by profligate social spending.** The economic slowdowns of 1982 and 1990 were both caused by the Bank of Canada's tough monetarist policies—the very anti-inflation strategy demanded by the bond-holders.

The new investor class still insists that, in order to lower government debt and deficits, we must reduce government spending even further rather than directly address the real causes—an inequitable tax system and high interest rates.

The fact is that deep government spending cuts have already been implemented. On a public accounts basis, that is the accounting method used by Finance Ministers in their budgets. In each of the five fiscal years 1987-88 through 1991-92, federal revenues were greater than program spending. In other words, there was a surplus on what is known as the "basic balance," that is the balance of revenues and program spending before debt service payments are taken into account.

Over those five years, the federal government took in $32 billion more than it spent on programs. Nevertheless, the debt grew from $272 billion in 1987 to $424 billion in 1992 because of growing public debt charges.

If we use a more comprehensive measure, the national accounts, we get a truer picture of the government's actual revenue and spending. This is so because the national accounts include several "off budget" sources of revenue such as profits from Crown corporations and interest earned on loans made by the federal government. On a national accounts basis, there has been an operating surplus every year from 1986 through 1995.[67]

As Chart Seven shows, even as the federal deficit is projected to decline over the fiscal years 1995-96 to 1997-98 by Finance Minister Paul Martin's 1996 budget, public debt charges are projected to continue to rise.

Chart Seven
Federal Deficits and Public Debt Charges
$ billions

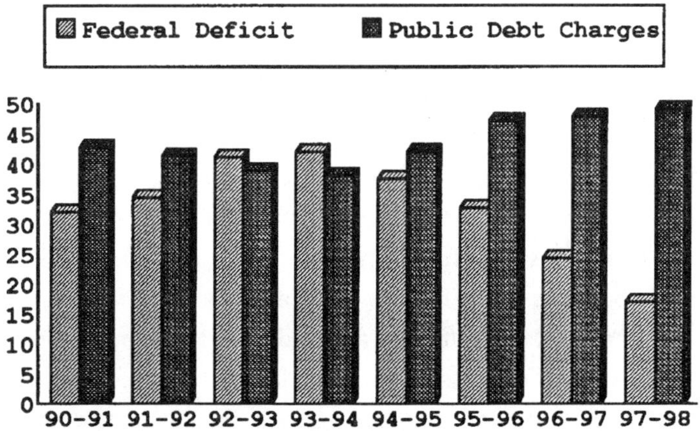

Source: 1996 Federal Budget

Putting The Deficit Cart Before the Interest Rate Horse

Finance Minister Paul Martin acknowledges the importance of bringing down interest rates. The Finance Minister correctly recognizes that, unless real interest rates come down below the rate of economic growth, he cannot bring the debt under control. As Martin put it in his document on A New Framework for Economic Policy, "When interest rates exceed the growth rate... the undertow of debt overpowers the buoyancy of growth and the debt ratio tends to rise exponentially."[68]

In his 1996 budget, Martin again reiterates the centrality of bringing down interest rates. But he never hints at any change in monetary policy. Martin says: "The best way to reduce interest rates is to continue to keep inflation low and get government deficits and debts under control."[69]

In effect, Martin insists on putting the deficit cart ahead of the interest rate horse. He bows to the power of the financial markets by saying that "high real interest rates reflect investors' concerns about governments' abilities to meet their financial commitments if they continue to run high deficits, combined more recently with political uncertainty...[an oblique reference to the Quebec referendum]." Martin goes on to say: "As a result [of high federal and provincial debts relative to GDP] investors in both Canada and the rest of the world demand a risk premium on money lent to Canadian governments... The bottom line is that, in order to get low long-term real interest rates consistent with low inflation, Canada's high debt-to-GDP ratio must be reduced."[70]

Aside from a few modest tax increases, Martin chooses to fight the deficit chiefly through spending cuts. The first three budgets Martin tabled since becoming Finance Minister will raise $12 billion in new revenue and cut spending by a total of $79 billion over the fiscal years 1994-95 through 1998-99.[71] But most of the money saved this way gets eaten up by increased public debt charges. In fact, over the fiscal years 1993-94 through 1997-98, increases in the cost of servicing the federal debt will more than wipe out all the projected savings on program spending.[71]

Over the eight months following the release of the 1996 budget, the Bank of Canada did succeed in lowering interest rates two percentage points below the projections set out in the budget. Professional bond traders say Canadian rates fell because governments continued to slash spending; inflation stayed low and the prospect of another Quebec referendum receded into the future. They seldom point to another important factor—the fact that the Canadian economy has been so flattened by high unemployment and the effects of government spending cuts that there was an urgent need for financial stimulation. So much so that the Governor of the Bank of Canada, Gordon Thiessen, had begun to talk not about the danger of renewed inflation, but about the opposite—the risk of deflation, that is, falling prices as occurred during the 1930s.

In fact, as previously noted, the Bank of Canada had become so alarmed about the lack of growth and the danger of deflation that it cut its overnight lending rate 17 times between June of 1995 and October 2, 1996. These rate cuts did not spark massive capital flight or a run on the Canadian dollar, in large part because lenders, including prominent bank economists, recognized that the Canadian economy needed stimulus. Despite the fact that short-term Canadian interest rates fell below U.S. rates, there was no flight of capital to the U.S., partly because inflation there remained one-and-a-half percentage points higher than in Canada.

How The Bank of Canada Surrendered to the Bond-holders

The weakness of our central bank in the face of private money markets is largely a self-inflicted debility. The Bank of Canada has all but abandoned efforts to influence bond markets. It no longer intervenes by buying and selling long-term bonds in the open market. Our central bank has also reduced its purchases and sales of three-month Treasury bills. Moreover, in 1991 the Mulroney government further reduced its powers by eliminating the requirement that private banks keep a minimum level of reserves with the Bank of Canada.

The accompanying box, entitled "How Money is Created," explains the relationship between money created by the Bank of Canada and the multiplication of the money supply through the private banking system. The box also explains why it is important to reinstate reserve requirements if we are to have democratic control over our money supply.

How Money is Created

Although we use money every day, we seldom ask where it comes from. Few people realize that most of the money we use is actually created by the banking system, and not issued by the government or the Bank of Canada.

Take a look at any paper money in your wallet and you will find the words "This note is legal tender." Only the Bank of Canada, our central bank wholly owned by the federal government, issues legal tender.

What this means is that if you owe someone $20 and you give her a $20 bill she has to accept it or the debt is absolved. On the other hand she doesn't have to accept your cheque drawn on a bank or a trust company if she doesn't want to. She can insist on being paid in legal tender.

A useful description for Bank of Canada legal tender is "right of purchase money" to distinguish it from the "promise to pay legal tender money" created by the private banks.

Now about 96% of the money we use is not legal tender but private banks' promise-to-pay legal tender money. This is what a bank creates for you when you take out a loan and promise to repay it at a certain rate of interest. The bank will give you legal tender if you really insist, but it knows that you'll settle for a cheque to go into your chequing account. You then use this account to send the bank's promise of legal tender to the folks from whom you make a purchase.

How Money is Created

(cont'd from previous page)

These folks in turn will deposit your cheque in another bank. They will use their account to write another cheque.

This same process occurs over and over again. The result is that only about 4% of the total money supply is legal tender. If the Bank of Canada were to create a larger fraction, of the money supply and the private banks a smaller fraction it would help greatly to bring down interest rates.

An essential point to understand is that once a bank has you sign a loan agreement (your promise to pay) and gives you a loan (its promise to pay), the money supply of Canada increases at that moment. As you repay your loan, the money supply shrinks. So money is being created and destroyed every day--by far the most of it by the private banks.

Every time a bank makes a loan (by creating a deposit in the account of the borrower) and the borrower spends the money she has borrowed (by writing cheques on the newly created deposit), some other bank receives a deposit on the money spent. That bank can lend out the deposit it has received, and thus additional new deposits are created in other banks; and as the process is repeated, more and more new money is created--many times greater than the total amount of cash deposited in all the banks.

In short, the banking system has the ability to greatly multiply the amount of money deposited with it. The multiplier factor is determined by how much of their deposits the banks elect (or are required through government reserve requirements) to retain in cash to cover the withdrawals clients may wish to make. The present reserve ratio used by Canadian banks is about 4%. Using this ratio, the banking system can create new money to a total of 25 times any new deposit money received.

The federal government can reduce (or increase) the multiplier factor through the use of reserve requirements. It used to do just that until the Mulroney government quietly removed such requirements in 1991. Reserve requirements can increase the deposit reserve ratio and require that some reserves be held in deposits with the Bank of Canada. If, for example, the deposit reserve requirement were set at 5%,the banks could only use a multiplier of 20, instead of the 25-fold increase that now occurs.

Such a larger reserve requirement could be used to offset any inflationary tendency that might result from decisions to have the Bank of Canada hold more federal government debt or make low-interest loans to the provinces. Thus any danger of the private banks putting too much money into circulation, and thus causing inflation, would be averted.

Source: adapted from an article by Jack Biddell in the <u>CCPA Monitor</u> February 1995

Since the middle of 1994, the Bank of Canada no longer views intervention in weekly auctions of three-month Treasury bills as its key monetary policy tool. Instead it is content to let the interest rate paid on short-term T-bills be set by private investors. The Bank used to intervene actively in these auctions as a way of influencing its own Bank Rate (charged on its loans to commercial banks) and thereby all other interest rates. The Bank Rate used to be set at a quarter of a percentage point above the value of three-month Treasury bills. Now the Bank of Canada "allows the three-month rate to move in response to market forces."[73]

At present, the only interest rate that the Bank of Canada sets directly is the "overnight loan rate" which is charged on the accounts the chartered banks use nightly to clear millions of dollars in payments to each other. This overnight rate effectively plays the same role as the former Bank Rate.

Although the ability to set the overnight rate is an important policy tool, the Bank of Canada has become much weaker than it used to be. Bank of Canada Governor Gordon Thiessen explains the Bank's current position in the following terms:

"The widely held view that the Bank of Canada controls the spectrum of interest rates in Canada... is a holdover from the days when the financial markets here and elsewhere were subject to controls and restrictions of various sorts... These days, markets are more open, more international and, as a result, much more efficient. [This means] that interest rates are more variable, and rates in Canada will move around in response to international events or domestic developments that alter market expectations.

"However, this does not imply that the market controls interest rates and the Bank has no capacity to pursue a monetary policy geared to Canadian requirements... The Bank has a direct effect on very short-term rates and through them an influence on the exchange rate. Our main effect on longer-term rates occurs indirectly through our influence on market expectations regarding inflation. These influences are sufficient for the Bank to carry out an independent monetary policy to control inflation."[74]

Consider carefully what Thiessen is saying. He is saying that the Bank can successfully carry out an independent monetary policy to fight inflation, which is exactly what the bond-holders want. **But he never claims that the Bank can buck the market and bring down interest rates faster or farther than the bond-holders want.**

A study by an economist at the Bank's financial markets department concluded that three recent efforts by the Bank to lower interest rates all backfired. The study looked at three occasions when the Bank did try to lower interest rates—in 1990, 1992 and 1994-95 after the Mexican peso crisis. In each case investors reacted by selling so many Treasury bills and bonds that interest rates rose dramatically, frustrating the Bank's efforts. The study concludes that "the Bank may have considerable difficulty achieving an easing (or preventing a tightening) in monetary conditions when its assessment of the outlook for the economy and inflation differs from that of the market."[75]

In other words, the Bank doubts whether it ever can lower rates without the cooperation of the bond-traders. Instead of trying to influence the markets, the Bank's governors argue that the best it can do is to adopt transparent policies and reassure traders that it will only intervene decisively to fight inflation. Thus the Bank of Canada's policy is biased in favour of tight money, high real interest rates, and high unemployment.

However, we draw a different lesson from the same episodes of failed attempts to lower rates. In our view the Bank did not go far enough in its efforts or even use all of the tools at its disposal.

What Needs to be Done

To become an effective policy-maker in a world of speculative capitalism, the Bank of Canada must reclaim all the policy leverage at its disposal. Most of the ideas presented here are drawn from the Alternative Federal Budget for 1996. The Alternative Budget was written by a working group of socially concerned Canadians, led by the Canadian Centre for Policy Alternatives and CHO!CES, a Manitoba coalition for social justice. We in the Ecumenical Coalition for Economic Justice have also been actively engaged in the Alternative Federal Budget for several years.

First of all, the Bank should use the power it still has to set the overnight rate to begin to nudge real interest rates down. In the Alternative

Budget we argue that the Bank should engineer reductions in average interest rates by reducing the target band within which the overnight lending rate floats.

If the bond traders attempt to frustrate such moves, then the Bank must be prepared to re-enter both the three-month Treasury bill and longer-term bond markets.

The accompanying box draws on the work of Prof. Gideon Rosenbluth to explain how a more active Bank of Canada might operate. Rosenbluth shows why the Bank must be willing to buy and hold a larger share of government debt. The 1996 Alternative Budget suggests that the bank "increase its holding of federal bonds by an amount equivalent to 2% of outstanding net debt per year for each of the next five years."

The Bank of Canada should return to holding approximately the same proportion of federal debt as it held in 1980. The amount of federal debt held by the Bank of Canada has grown relatively little over the last 15 years, rising from $16.1 billion in 1980 to only $23.6 billion at the end of 1995. As Chart Eight shows, in relative terms the share of the national debt held by the Bank of Canada has fallen dramatically from 19.5% of total federal government debt in 1980 to only 5.1% in 1995. Meanwhile, the amount of federal debt held abroad has risen from $9 billion in 1980 to $119.5 billion at the end of 1995. The share held by non-residents has risen from 10.9% to 26% of the total over the same period.

What if non-resident bond-holders respond by dumping Canadian debt? The Alternative Budget suggests two options for increasing the domestic demand for federal bonds. First, the government could require that Registered Pension Plans (RPPs) and Registered Retirement Savings Plans (RRSPs) invest a minimum proportion of their portfolios in government bonds as a condition for receiving their tax deductibility. This measure has enormous potential, since at the end of 1993 RPPs held $424 billion while RRSPs were worth $177 billion.

Secondly, the government could gradually lower the ceiling on allowable foreign investments by RPPs and RRSPs. The Mulroney government raised this quota to 20% from 10% through gradual increments of 2% per annum. By the end of 1994, these retirement funds had invested about 13% of their assets abroad, up from 5% in 1990. If these funds were repatriated in roughly equal instalments over 13 years, it would generate about $6 billion a year of new demand for Canadian bonds or equity investments.

Chart Eight

Holdings of Federal Government Debt

percent of total

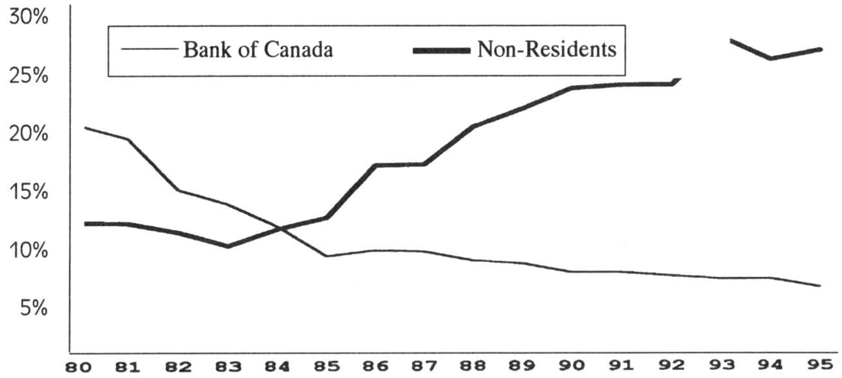

Source: Bank of Canada Review

How the Bank of Canada Could Lower Interest Rates

Gideon Rosenbluth, professor emeritus of economics from the University of British Columbia, provides the following explanation of how the Bank of Canada could lower interest rates by intervening in loan markets.

The Bank of Canada can buy and sell both 90-day Treasury bills and longer-term government bonds in the open market. But in recent years it has reduced its activity in the Treasury bill market and stayed out of the market for longer-term bonds.

If the Bank wants to lower interest rates, it can buy more Treasury bills and hold them in its own portfolio. The increased demand these purchases generate tends to increase prices, and a rise in prices of Treasury bills means a drop in their yield (i.e. the rate of interest that a purchaser will earn). Conversely, to raise interest rates, the bank can sell Treasury bills.

Although the Bank may only intervene in one market, the various credit markets are all connected, since lenders and borrowers can substitute one kind

How the Bank of Canada Could Lower Interest Rates

(Continued from previous page)

of debt for another. "So, if the bank lowers Treasury bill yields, it exerts downward pressure on the interest yields of federal and provincial bonds, corporate bonds, bank loans, mortgages, guaranteed investment certificates, annuities, and so on. Of course, this indirect influence on bond rates is weaker than if the Bank intervened in these markets directly, as it has done in the past. In staying out of the bond market, the bank has abandoned a powerful policy tool."

Some argue that interest rates cannot be lowered because Canadian interest rates are determined by world (read US) interest rates. As fast as the Bank of Canada's purchases raise the demand, foreign and domestic lenders will increase the supply. These bondholders will sell their Canadian bonds and buy US securities. Moreover, at lower rates Canadian governments will not find new lenders to replace maturing debt or buy new bond issues because the potential lenders would do better by investing their money in the United States. Or so the argument goes.

Rosenbluth replies that this argument is unrealistic because it assumes that "no matter how much the Bank buys, the supply will increase to meet the demand **without a rise in price."** But some holders of Canadian bonds will not sell unless the price rises. Others will hold on to their Canadian bonds because investment in foreign bonds exposes them to a foreign exchange risk. Some Canadian bond owners will have already reached the limits of foreign holdings permitted by the regulations governing retirement savings plans. "But the most important point is that lenders, both foreign and domestic, differ widely in the amount and quality of information they possess concerning the risks of different debt instruments, foreign and domestic, in their interpretation of this information, and in their attitude to risk.

"Consequently, as interest rates drop, that is, as security prices rise, some foreign lenders will sell some or all of their holdings of Canadian government debt; **others will not sell.** The higher the price in relation to other investment opportunities, the more will be offered for sale. Consequently, the Bank of Canada can indeed raise the price by intervening in the market to buy and hold more government debt. **The lower the interest rate that is to be achieved, the more of the debt the Bank must hold."**

adapted from: Gideon Rosenbluth in Osberg and Fortin (1996) p.102-105.

Is Bank of Canada Intervention Inevitably Inflationary?

Table Three

Monetized Government Debt as a Percentage of the Money Supply and the Rate of Inflation

Year	Percentage of Money Supply	Rate of Inflation GNE deflator
1989	7.5%	3.6
1985	8.3%	3.2
1980	10.9%	11.4
1975	11.1%	10.7
1970	13.6%	4.6
1965	17.5%	3.3
1960	19.7%	1.3
1955	21.2%	0.6
1950	22.9%	2.4

Source: H. Chorney, "The provinces Should Have Access to the Bank of Canada," (Ottawa: The Canadian Centre for Policy Alternatives, 1992)

The investor class will argue that any additional purchases of government debt by the Bank of Canada will only be "monetizing" the debt, equivalent to printing money. Since monetarists view inflation as the consequence of "too much money chasing too few goods," they say that monetizing the debt is inevitably inflationary.

The historical record, however, does not support this view. In Table Three, Prof. Harold Chorney shows how in the past the central bank held much larger shares of the federal debt without creating inflation.

Michael Bradfield, an economist at Dalhousie University, shows how the Bank of Canada could offset any inflationary effect monetizing more debt might have by raising the reserve requirement on deposits held by financial institutions. Higher reserves would have the effect of reducing the money supply by an equivalent amount to what is added when the Bank monetizes government debt. For this strategy to be effective, the reserve requirements, removed by the Mulroney government in 1991, would have to be restored.

Holding more debt through the Bank of Canada has an additional benefit. All the profits earned by the Bank would eventually revert to the federal treasury. At the end of each fiscal year the Bank totals up its income, deducts its operating expenses, and turns over all its profits to the federal government.

Canadians Demand Action

We should not underestimate the difficulties involved in the strategy we propose. The Finance Minister and the Bank of Canada Governor may have to co-ordinate their actions with similar efforts by their counterparts in other countries to avoid destabilizing capital flight. As we shall see in Chapter Five, in this age of speculative capitalism states must work together in pursuit of lower real interest rates and the regulation of finance capital.

When given an opportunity to choose between the actual policies of the federal government and the more socially responsible proposals of the Alternative Budget, Canadians overwhelmingly prefer the Alternative. Sixty-four per cent of Canadians surveyed by a Vector poll preferred the 1995 Alternative Budget's emphasis on job creation, lower interest rates and higher corporate taxes to the Liberal government's reliance on spending cuts and layoffs to reduce the deficit.[76] A similar poll conducted in 1996 found that 61% of those surveyed preferred that year's Alternative Budget.

In the spring of 1996, thousands of Canadians, led by the women's movement and women within the labour movement, marched and demonstrated throughout the country. The six weeks of actions culminated with a March on Parliament Hill on June 8. Their cry was "For Bread and Roses, For Jobs and Justice". Couched in this overall slogan were 15 specific demands reproduced in the box below that called upon the federal government to renew its responsibility for the elimination of poverty through the creation of jobs and raising the minimum hourly wage to $7.85.

Call to Action

Roses:

The National Action Committee on the Status of Women (NAC) and the Canadian Labour Congress (CLC) have come together to organize a Women's March Against Poverty: For Bread and Roses! For Jobs and Justice!

We recognize that Aboriginal peoples and the people of Quebec have distinct needs which must be respected in all programs brought in by the federal government. We reject the suggestion that respecting the unique needs of these communities requires off-loading federal responsibility for social programs in the rest of Canada onto provincial and municipal governments and onto individual families.

Our vision of Canada is a multi-cultural, multiracial society without discrimination based on sex, race, national origin, disability or sexual orientation.

We are marching to bring about a society based on social solidarity, not social exclusion.

Jobs:

We are calling for jobs with a future, for women.
We are calling for the minimum wage to be raised immediately to $7.85 per hour.
We are calling for access by Aboriginal women to federal employment and training resources.

Bread:

We are calling for a Canada Social Security Act.
We are calling for the promised national child care program.
We are calling for guaranteed, portable and secure support programs for people with disabilities.
We are calling for the strengthening of the public pension system and maintaining women's independent access to old age benefits.
We are calling for the enforcement of the Canada Health Act.
We are calling for post-secondary education to be accessible to women through grants not loans.
We are calling for the surplus in the UI fund to be used to restore benefit levels.
We are calling for the creation of 14,000 units of social housing a year.

Justice:

We are calling for $40 million for feminist services against male violence.
We are calling for the end to the sexist, racist and anti-poor $975 head tax.
We are calling for the inclusion of sexual orientation as prohibited grounds for discrimination in the Canadian Human Rights Act.
We are calling for the elimination of women's poverty to be a foreign policy objective.

Similar actions have been taken under the leadership of women in Québec. Their first March Against Poverty took place a year earlier in protest of the policies of the Parti Quebecois that are similar to those of the federal government in Ottawa.

The voices of protest declare that the policies being followed by the government are not for the good of the people, and are not what Canadians elected their governments to do. They reject government policies that reflect the priorities of international investors. Above all, the Canadian people do not accept the Prime Minister's assertion that there is nothing that can be done in the face of pressures from international finance.

CHAPTER FOUR

Mexico Swamped By A Whirlpool of Speculation

Mexicans call it simply "the crisis". Since the dramatic devaluation of the peso in December of 1994, Mexicans have suffered enormous income and job losses. Per capita income fell by 8.5% in 1995. In that same year, 908,000 jobs disappeared from the formal economy, while over a million youths entered the work-force. Three-quarters of the 24 million people who live in rural Mexico now live in poverty, while one-third, 8.8 million, live in extreme poverty.

Young women toiling in Mexico's export-processing factories, known as *maquiladoras*, saw the real purchasing power of their wages fall by about 28% since January of 1994. In September of 1995 the minimum wage was only sufficient to buy one-third of a basic food basket without taking into account housing, transportation, health, education and recreation.[77]

The story of how the Mexican economy crashed illustrates the contradictions of speculative capitalism. Almost three-quarters of the US$98.5 billion of foreign investment that flowed into Mexico over the years 1989 to 1994 was short-term portfolio investment. All this foreign money artificially raised the value of the peso. But these large capital inflows, which financed Mexico's trade deficit and foreign debt service payments, were unsustainable. They did not generate much new revenue because only about 15% of the new money was invested in production.[78]

The turnaround occurred in 1994 after some foreign investors were frightened away by a combination of events. Political turmoil, including the January 1st, 1994 uprising by the Zapatista Army of National Liberation (EZLN) in Chiapas, caused some foreign investors to withdraw their money. The assassinations of the official Institutional Revolutionary Party's (PRI) presidential candidate, Luis Donaldo Colosio, and other prominent politicians, judges and Cardinal Juan Jesús Posadas caused further concern.

Some investors were scared off by an article in *Fortune* entitled "It's Time to Get Real About Mexico".[79] The article exposed the influence of the illicit drug cartels and warned investors about systemic corruption.

Investment also dried up because rising interest rates in the U.S. during 1994 made investing there more attractive. Many Mexican commentators had predicted that a devaluation was inevitable as the government resorted to drawing down its foreign exchange reserves to cover its trade deficit and debt service costs.

In the first year after the peso was devalued, nervous investors took US$27.5 billion out of the country, leaving the Mexican people to cope with a devastating crisis. The US$50 billion rescue package organized by the Clinton administration and the International Monetary Fund (IMF) left Mexico with an even heavier burden of foreign debt.

The Mexican government, the IMF and the World Bank all acknowledge that too much speculation and too little real investment brought on the crisis. An IMF study of the causes of the Mexican debacle even includes a recommendation that emerging markets, like Mexico, should favour foreign direct investment over portfolio investment.[80]

The World Bank's assessment of lessons from the crisis states: "The composition of capital inflows is very important... Keeping speculative capital under control, while encouraging long-term investment—as Chile has done— makes eminent sense. Increasing the share of long-term investment funds, however, will not be easy."[81]

Neither the IMF nor the World Bank ever explains how the share of direct investment might be increased. Neither body draws attention to the fact that the North American Free Trade Agreement (NAFTA) prohibits any kind of performance requirement that might be used to channel foreign investment away from speculation and into productive endeavours.

The Mexican experience is a clear example of what can happen when the financial economy is privileged over the real economy. NAFTA was supposed to have improved Mexico's real economic prospects. In actual fact, most of the money that came into Mexico was speculative "cybermoney" that was never invested in anything tangible. Mexico's crisis lucidly demonstrates the vulnerability of heavily indebted countries to volatile international capital flows. Recognizing the role that fly-by-night capital played in the crisis, Alan Greenspan, chairperson of the U.S. Federal Reserve Board, astutely calls Mexico "the first casualty of the new international financial system."[82]

Although Canada has not fallen into an extreme crisis like Mexico, there are more parallels between our two countries' financial difficulties than might at first seem obvious. We begin our analysis by looking back at the origins of Mexico's financial crisis.

Failure of Tax Reform Started Debt Ball Rolling

The roots of Mexico's financial crisis can be traced to failed efforts at tax reform during the early 1970s, the same years that the seeds of Canada's debt and deficit problems were sown through tax concessions given to big business and wealthy investors.

In Mexico, President Luis Echeverria (1970-1976) tried to reform a very regressive and corrupt tax system. When Echeverria took office, Mexico had one of the lowest income taxes in the world. Tax evasion was rampant as the upper class bought off tax collectors with bribes or hid their wealth by buying real estate and opening bank accounts in the United States. Echeverria tried to increase taxes on corporations and upper income earners.

Business organizations and the wealthy fought back with a capital strike. The rich deposited more money abroad. Big business formed the Co-ordinating Council of Businessmen (CCE) as a united front against Echeverria's policies and refused to invest. Echeverria responded by expanding public investment. He increased the number of state enterprises from 84 in 1970 to 845 by 1976. As a result, government spending also rose over the same period from 23.6% to 36.6% of GDP.[83]

But tax reform did not produce sufficient revenue to pay for the new spending, so Echeverria took the fateful decision to borrow abroad. The external public debt quadrupled from US$4.9 billion in 1970 to US$19.6 billion in 1976. Total external debt that year, including that of private corporations and banks, was US$26.1 billion.[84]

Echeverria's excessive borrowing led to a balance of payments crisis. In 1976 Mexico went cap in hand to the International Monetary Fund (IMF), which imposed stiff conditions on a bail-out. The austerity program included devaluation of the peso, wage controls, and cutbacks in government spending in return for stand-by credits from the IMF.

Echeverria's successor, José Lopez Portillo (1976-1982), secured new private loans for the state oil company, Pemex, by announcing previously undisclosed data concerning Mexico's oil reserves. In a flurry of announcements spread over Lopez Portillo's six-year term, official estimates of Mexico's petroleum reserves kept growing from 11.2 billion barrels in 1976 to 72 billion barrels in 1982.

At the time, we in ECEJ invoked our own Canadian experience with overblown petroleum reserve estimates to warn Mexicans to be wary of artificially inflated figures that serve corporate or government interests.[85] Later, Francisco Inguanzo, a retired Pemex petroleum engineer, confirmed that the data had indeed been falsified.[86]

In 1977 Mexico's Finance Minister confidently told New York bankers that "Oil will be the turning point of the Mexican economy."[87] Based on the promise of increased oil exports, foreign banks eagerly lent more money to Pemex, raising its debt from US$3 billion in 1977 to US$20 billion in 1981. The Federal Electricity Commission owed another US$10 billion. Thus the two energy companies were responsible for more than half of Mexico's foreign debt of US$53 billion at the end of 1981. This debt was three times as large as it had been in 1976 at the end of Echeverria's term.

Banks Anxious to Lend

In the wake of the 1973 and 1979 petroleum price increases, private banks were flush with deposits from member countries of the Organization of Petroleum Exporting Countries (OPEC) and anxious to lend. During the mid- to late-1970s, the cost of servicing international bank loans was low, especially for oil-exporting countries like Mexico. The real interest rate paid on these loans may be estimated by subtracting the price index for primary commodity exports by less developed countries from the nominal interest rate. Here we use the London Inter-Bank Offered Rate (Libor) as a benchmark for international lending.

Although this is not as precise as the calculation used for estimating real interest rates in Canada in the previous chapters, it serves as a general indication of the cost of international borrowing by less developed countries. (The measure is less precise because the price index used covers a variety of commodities, while an individual country's exports may be concentrated in one or two kinds of merchandise whose prices may be above or below the general index.)

This calculation shows that the real interest rate paid on international bank loans to less developed countries averaged only 0.5% a year between 1975 and 1979. At the time no one foresaw that the U.S. Federal Reserve Board was about to make what, in retrospect, was one of the most fateful decisions of this century. In October of 1979, the U.S. central bank adopted monetarism as the official U.S. monetary policy.

Technically, this meant that the U.S. was determined to fight inflation by restricting the money supply. In fact, the Federal Reserve Board's real concern was growing speculation against the U.S. dollar and complaints by financiers about low returns generally.[88] The consequence of this decision was an increase in American, and soon international, interest rates.

The ensuing rise in interest rates brought on the Great Recession of 1981-82 in the United States and Canada. The recession also reduced demand, and therefore prices, for primary commodity exports, including oil. As a result, the real interest rate paid on international bank loans to less developed countries (Libor minus the commodity price index) soared from an average of 0.5% over the years 1975 to 1979 to an average of 8.3% over the years 1980 to 1994. Moreover, real interest rates have remained above their historical levels ever since. As Michael Moffitt observed, "Usury was institutionalized."[89]

The 1982 Mexican debt crisis was a direct consequence of the change in U.S. monetary policy. The crisis sent shock waves through world financial markets. Bankers knew that a default by Mexico could have set off a chain reaction that would have caused the failure of even the largest private banks. Mexico played a pivotal role throughout the Third World debt crisis of the 1980s.

In our earlier studies, *Debt Bondage or Self Reliance* (1985) and *Recolonization or Liberation* (1990), we showed how Mexico became a showcase for International Monetary Fund and World Bank Structural Adjustment Programs (SAPs).

The 1994-95 Mexican crisis provides conclusive proof that rigorous adherence to orthodox SAPs failed to resolve the 1982 debt crisis. In 1994-95, just as in 1982, the chief response to the crisis has been to offer new emergency financing conditional on the acceptance of harsh austerity measures. In both cases, the new credits did not address the root causes. Instead they only added to the mountain of unpayable debt. As the box entitled "Lurching From Crisis to Crisis" shows, the debt restructurings that occurred in 1985, 1987 and 1990 also failed to resolve the underlying problems.

Lurching From Crisis to Crisis

Year	Event	External Debt at Year end (US$billions)
1976	Mexico Negotiates Austerity Agreement with the IMF	$26.1
1982	Mexico's Near Default Starts Latin American Debt Crisis	$86.2
1985	$48 billion of Mexican Debt Restructured Under the Baker Plan (named after US Treasury Secretary James Baker)	$101.6
1987	$45 billion Mexican Debt Again Restructured	$107.5
1990	$37 billion of Mexican Debt Restructured Under the Brady Plan (named after US Treasury Secretary Nicholas Brady)	$98.2
Jan. 1, 1994	NAFTA Takes Effect - EZLN Rebels Against "Death Sentence" for Mexico's Poor and Indigenous People	$117.6 (end of 1993)
Dec. 20, 1994	Peso Devaluation Marks New Financial Crisis	$140.1
Feb. 1995	Clinton Administration and IMF Announce $50 billion Bail-Out	$173 (end of 1995)

The amount of debt relief available under the Baker and Brady debt relief plans was never sufficient. Chart Nine shows how some minor declines in total debt also occurred in 1989 and 1992. Neither of these reductions was the result of debt relief by Mexico's creditors. The 1989 decrease was due to the cancellation of some debts in conjunction with the privatization of some state enterprises and some swapping of debt for equity investments. The 1992 decline in total debt was achieved through the repurchase of debt from the secondary market.

Chart Nine

Mexico's External Debt 1980 - 1995

US$ billions

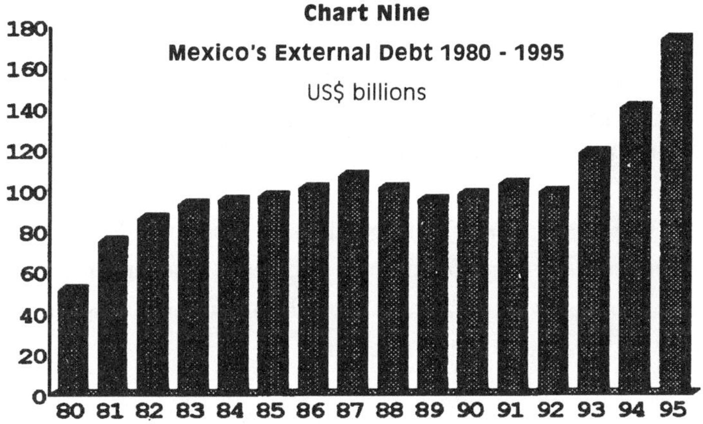

Source: Mexican Action Network on Free Trade

IMF Medicine Privileged the Financial Sector

The 1982 crisis was never resolved, in part because the austerity medicine prescribed by the IMF on behalf of all Mexico's creditors chiefly benefited the financial sector at the expense of the productive economy. Austerity measures squeezed internal demand while export revenues were eaten up by debt service payments and unavailable for investment in development.

Carlos Salinas de Gortari, first as Planning Minister under President Miguel de la Madrid (1982-1988) and later as President (1988-1994), was the architect of much of the economic restructuring that took place in Mexico over those 12 years. As President, Salinas ingenuously declared that the debt crisis was over and that by joining NAFTA Mexico was on the road to becoming a developed country.

However, all the time that Salinas was President, a deeper financial crisis was brewing. For one thing, the nature of Mexico's external debt was changing. After 1982 the big international banks stopped making new loans to Mexico and sold off many of their existing loans. In 1990 they converted many of their loans into so-called "Brady bonds". Named after U.S. Treasury Secretary Nicholas Brady, these bonds replaced about US$40 billion worth of Mexican government debt owed to commercial banks.

Under the Brady Plan, the banks had the choice of two different kinds of Brady bonds. Some banks opted to trade about US$22.5 billion in bank debt for undiscounted 30-year bonds paying 6.25% fixed interest. Other banks chose to swap about US$17.8 billion worth of existing debt, at a discount of 35% off face value, for 30-year bonds with floating interest rates.

Ever since, these Brady bonds have been bought and sold on the open market. The rise and fall of their prices acts as a barometer of investor confidence in Mexico. In March of 1996 a Brady bond futures market opened up on the Chicago Mercantile Exchange.[90]

Mutual Funds Replaced Banks

Since it could no longer count on bank credit, Mexico started borrowing from other sources such as the mutual funds and pension funds described in Chapter Two of this study. In 1981, bank loans made up 77% of the foreign investment in such "emerging markets" as Mexico, Brazil, Chile, Argentina and Sri Lanka. By 1993, 74% of private foreign investment in these countries came from mutual funds and pension funds.[91]

Faced with a growing trade deficit resulting from its trade liberalization policies and continued high debt service costs, the Salinas government did everything possible to keep foreign funds flowing into Mexico. First they attracted foreign investment (and lured back some of the capital that wealthy Mexicans had stashed abroad) through the privatization of state enterprises.

Salinas reversed Echeverria's public ownership policies by privatizing 269 state-owned companies between 1989 and 1994. Unfortunately, most of the income went to making external debt payments instead of social or economic development, as had been promised. The privatizations led to significant job losses as some 400,000 positions were eliminated by the new owners.[92]

A second strategy pursued by Salinas involved deregulation of the Mexican stock market, known as the Bolsa, opening it up to foreign investors. At first this strategy succeeded in attracting foreign purchases of non-controlling shares in newly privatized firms like Telmex, the giant telephone company. Control over Telmex remained firmly in the hands of a small group of investors who were the President's friends (and some say stand-ins or what the Mexicans call *prestanombres* for the real beneficiary, Carlos Salinas).

Between 1988 and 1994, the Mexican Bolsa rose a thousand points, reflecting speculation in share prices out of all proportion to the real worth of company assets. Alejandro Alvarez estimates that, over the six years of Salinas's rule, speculators increased the nominal value of their portfolios by some US$100 billion by buying and selling the shares of privatized firms on the Bolsa.[93]

But this kind of investment did not generate new economic activity or new jobs, just changes of ownership. Telmex shares proved profitable because the government allowed the newly privatized firm to raise local phone rates without any real improvement in service.

The third strategy was to attract foreign investment into purchases of government bonds by offering very high interest rates. Initially, investors bought a type of Mexican bond known as the *cete*. But purchases of peso-denominated *cetes* declined as buyers became wary of the losses they might incur in the event of a devaluation.

The Salinas government then invented a new type of financial instrument, the *tesobono. Tesobonos* are Mexican government bonds nominally denominated in pesos but effectively indexed to the U.S. dollar exchange rate. This puts the risk of losses due to a devaluation on the Mexican government rather than the bond-holder. By the end of 1994, the Mexican government had US$28 billion worth of *tesobonos* outstanding.

NAFTA's Role in the Crisis

The other major factor attracting foreign capital to Mexico was, of course, the signing of the North American Free Trade Agreement (NAFTA). Many investors were attracted to Mexico by NAFTA's guarantees against any kind of capital controls. NAFTA gave foreign speculators the right to take their money out at any time. It also enticed new investors, especially in mutual funds, who previously might not have invested in a less developed country, with a chance to make higher returns than could be made in North America.

Investments in emerging markets, like Mexico, earned average annual returns of 19% between 1989 and 1994, compared to the 10.5% that could have been earned by investing in the stocks listed on the Standard and Poor's index.[94]

The Mexican Action Network on Free Trade (known by its Spanish acronym RMALC) notes how NAFTA played a central role in the genesis of the crisis. NAFTA must be understood as an instrument designed to make permanent the neoliberal structural adjustment policies of the Salinas government. Indeed, the U.S. Ambassador to Mexico, John Negroponte, made NAFTA's true mission clear in a 1991 memo he wrote to the US State Department, which was leaked to the newsmagazine Proceso:

"[NAFTA] can be seen as an instrument to promote, consolidate and guarantee continued policies of economic reform in Mexico beyond the Salinas administration... I think it's reasonable to suppose that the [NAFTA] negotiations themselves will be a useful lever in prying open the Mexican economy even further. For example, I think we can ... expect the foreign investment law to change...[and] liberalization of the financial services regime."[95]

The investment and financial services chapters in NAFTA have indeed had enormous consequences for Mexico. For one thing, they facilitate speculation by removing the ability of governments to channel foreign investment into productive uses. The investment chapter in NAFTA prohibits performance requirements that would oblige foreign companies to hire Mexicans or use Mexican suppliers.

Article 1109 of the investment chapter (which also applies to financial transactions through Article 1401:2) prohibits any kind of restrictions on cross-border flows of all kinds of financial dealings, including profits, interest, dividends and fees.

NAFTA Article 2104 requires any member country with external payments problems to consult with the International Monetary Fund and adopt any measures the Fund might recommend. Mexico did just that during the peso crisis and found itself in a deep recession. The austerity measures that are integral to Structural Adjustment Programs (SAPs) diminish effective demand in the domestic market as people's incomes are squeezed.

NAFTA leaves Mexico without the tools it needs to confront the serious problem of volatile fly-by-night capital. Under NAFTA, Mexico has few policy levers to escape from the currents of speculative international capital flows. Ironically, one country that has successfully slowed down international speculation in recent years is NAFTA's prospective new member, Chile.

The World Bank notes approvingly that Chile is the only country in the Latin America and Caribbean region in which direct investment has predominated over portfolio investment in recent years.[96] However, the World Bank fails to point out one of the major reasons for this success. Chile has enacted a law that requires portfolio investments to remain within the country for a minimum of one year. Thanks to this law, Chile was buffeted less than other Latin American countries by the "tequila effect" that destabilized financial markets early in 1995 as nervous investors sought safe havens for their money in the wake of Mexico's troubles.

A law like the one in effect in Chile requiring that portfolio investments remain within the country for a minimum of one year would not be compatible with NAFTA's investment provisions. In the wake of Mexico's troubles, it would make sense to amend NAFTA to allow member countries, including Canada, to emulate Chile by requiring portfolio investors to hold their investments for longer periods. The Chilean example shows that national governments still can regulate capital flows if they have the tools to do the job.

Before NAFTA, the Salinas government promised that it would bring new foreign investment that would help to modernize industry. But since NAFTA prohibits all kinds of performance requirements, it is forbid-

Chart Ten

Mexican Content of Manufacturing Exports
(percentage of value-added including labour)

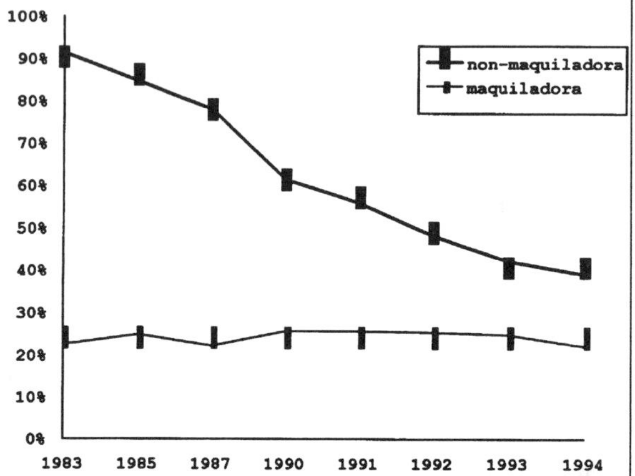

Source: Alberto Arroyo, Mexican Action Network on Free Trade

den for Mexico to require foreign investors to use Mexican inputs in production. As a result, the Mexican content of non-labour inputs used in *maquiladora* production fell from its historical average of 1.73% to only 1.45% in 1995. When labour is included in the calculation, the Mexican content of *maquiladora* exports was 22.1% in 1994, slightly below its historical level as shown in Chart Ten.

Trade liberalization has had a more dramatic effect on the Mexican content of non-*maquiladora* manufacturing exports. In the first year of NAFTA, the Mexican content of manufacturing exports by Mexican industry was only 39%, and half of that was labour. As Chart Ten shows, back in 1983, before Mexico embarked on trade liberalization, the national content of manufactured exports had been 91.4%.

Free trade has caused the few Mexican industries that prospered through increased exports to become disconnected from the rest of the national economy. Instead of becoming the motor of growth, the export sector used more and more imported inputs, thereby causing unemployment for the employees of its previous suppliers.

As the graph shows, only 39 cents of each dollar of Mexican non-*maquiladora* manufacturing exports and only 22 cents of each dollar of *maquila* exports remained in Mexico during 1994. When labour costs are taken out of the picture, only one-fifth of the value of non-*maquila* exports and 1.45% of the value added in *maquiladoras* represent purchases of goods from Mexican suppliers. Thus, the effect on employment in the rest of the economy is very small. Despite the increase in Mexican exports of manufactured goods, 77,839 jobs were lost from the non-*maquiladora* manufacturing sector during the first two years of NAFTA.

Pattern of Foreign Investment Changed

As a result of all these factors—privatization, deregulation of the stock exchange, high interest rates, protection against devaluation through *tesobonos,* and NAFTA's investment rules—the pattern of foreign investment flowing into Mexico began to change. As Table Four and Chart Eleven show, the share of direct foreign investment began to fall while the proportion of more speculative portfolio investment rose until 1994.

Even before the dramatic devaluation in December of 1994, wary and savvy investors were selling off their Mexican bonds. Between Jan. 1 and Nov. 23, 1994, new foreign investment on the Mexican stock market fell by 62.5%, while foreign investment in government bonds dropped by 80% as compared to the previous year.[97]

Table Four
Foreign Investment in Mexico 1989-1995
(US$ millions)

	1989	1990	1991	1992	1993	1994	1995
Total	3,527	6,004	17,515	22,443	33,308	16,166	-24,515
Direct	3,176	2,633	4,762	4,393	4,389	7,980	3,000
Portfolio	351	3,371	12,753	18,041	28,919	8,186	-27,515
of which							
stocks	493	1,995	6,332	4,783	10,717	4,088	-9,878
peso bonds			3,406	8,147	7,406	-2,225	} -17,637
dollar bonds	-142	1,376	3,015	5,111	10,797	6,342	

Sources: Compiled by Alberto Arroyo from the following:
Bank of Mexico Balance of Payments (revised). First Report of the Zedillo Government p.69.
June 1994 SECOFI (Ministry of Trade and Industrial Development) taken from La Jornada 16/02/95:47.
Jaime Zabludosky, Undersecretary for Trade, taken from La Jornada 10/11/95:50.
and Mexican Stock Exchange taken from La Jornada 10/01/96:47.

Chart Eleven
Foreign Investment in Mexico 1989 - 1995
(annual flows US$ billions)

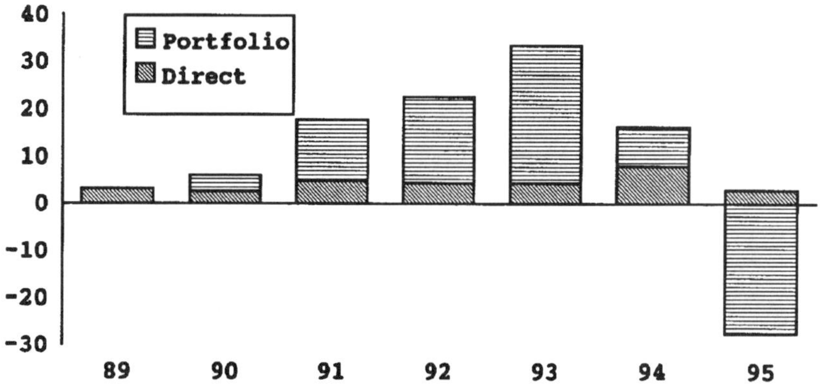

Source: derived from Table Four.

The Table and Chart show how new foreign direct investment (FDI) remained fairly constant, even growing to almost US$8 billion in 1994. What made total foreign investment so volatile was the inflow of portfolio investment which overtook FDI as early as 1990 but fell off during 1994 and then fled the country after the peso devaluation. In 1995, the net outflow of portfolio investment amounted to US$27.5 billion, which included US$9.9 billion that had been invested in shares on the stock market and US$17.6 billion worth of Mexican bonds.

All this foreign investment generated almost no employment. Over the years 1989 to 1994, 44% of the new foreign investment went to purchase government bonds, refinancing existing debt rather than creating any new jobs. Another 29% went to purchase shares in existing enterprises and therefore created few new jobs. Part of the remaining 27% in FDI went to buy out already existing companies and therefore did not add any new employment, either.[98]

The influx of speculative, fly-by-night capital precipitated the Dec. 1994 peso crisis by artificially creating a demand for pesos which was unsustainable and out of all proportion to the country's actual productive capacity. It created a false impression of a prosperous Mexico, when in fact the only sectors that were growing were a few export industries. Just 300 companies, the majority of which are transnationals, are responsible for 70% of Mexico's total exports.[99]

Propped up by the inflow of foreign capital, the peso was deliberately kept overvalued as part of Mexico's anti-inflation strategy. The overvalued peso made imports cheaper and thus helped keep prices in check.[100] The government did not devalue earlier for fear of the impact on the August 1994 Presidential election in which Ernesto Zedillo, the candidate of the official Institutional Revolutionary Party (PRI), succeeded Carlos Salinas.

When the devaluation did occur, it was badly mishandled. Some of Mexico's business elite were tipped off in a late night meeting with the Finance Minister, Jaime Serra Puche, on Dec. 19. When the meeting broke up at 4 a.m. on Dec. 20, many of those assembled called their brokers with instructions to sell pesos and buy dollars on the European markets.

What angered Wall St. and Bay St. money managers was how the Finance Minister had publicly insisted only a few days before that there would be no devaluation, while privately tipping off some of Mexico's wealthiest citizens. Accordingly, they demanded, and soon secured, Serra Puche's resignation.

While some foreign investors lost money because of the devaluation, other smart speculators made windfalls. Those who saw the devaluation coming made a lot of money by betting against the peso. For example, the John Henry currency speculation fund provided its clients with an extraordinary 3,240% annualized return on their investments during 10 days of the peso crisis.[101]

A Bailout for Speculators

Supposedly, investors earn very high returns on Mexican investments because of the risks they take. In fact, the rescue package organized by the Clinton administration and the IMF removed the risk.

After failing to get the U.S. Congress to cooperate, Clinton used his executive powers to approve a US$20 billion loan from the Exchange Stabilization Fund. Despite rantings by right-wing Republican foes of the

Clinton administration, the loan cannot be classified as foreign aid. Mexico has to pay fees that will rise each time it draws down the line of credit. In addition, it has to pay interest at the same rate as 91-day U.S. Treasury bills, plus a sizable risk premium of 2.25 to 3.75 percentage points.[102] Due to these fees and high interest rates, the US government will gain US$1.5 billion more than it would have collected if it had lent the money to its own citizens.[103]

Canada also put up a C$1.5 billion line of credit to support the peso. The IMF promised to lend Mexico up to US$17.8 billion, which is three-and-a-half times more than it ever lent to any other country during its 50-year history. "When the circumstances are exceptional, the support must be exceptional," explained the IMF's managing director, Michel Camdessus.[104]

The IMF chief warned that, if Mexico could not roll over its debts, it could have led to "a true world catastrophe," since other countries would have followed Mexico into default. Pressure on other countries would have come from nervous investors quickly withdrawing their funds for fear of exchange controls.

One of the prime beneficiaries of the bailout is Goldman Sachs and Company, the firm that Treasury Secretary Robert Rubin used to run before he was appointed to the Clinton cabinet. The *Wall Street Journal* reports that Goldman Sachs "ranked as the No. 1 underwriter of Mexican stocks and bonds on the U.S. and European markets for 1992 through 1994. In those three years ... Goldman underwrote US$5.17 billion in Mexican securities."[105]

The bailout would buoy the value of outstanding Mexican bonds and make future sales more secure for investment firms like Goldman Sachs. Other major beneficiaries include investment dealers J.P. Morgan (US$2 billion) and Bear Stearns (US$1.8 billion).

While investors are the big beneficiaries of the bailout, the people of Mexico are saddled with paying back an even larger debt.

Of the US$22 billion lent to Mexico in the first three months of 1995, only 5% went to finance productive investments or social spending. The remaining 95% simply went to reschedule the government's debt, much of it to buy back *tesobonos* from foreign investors. Previously approved credits from the World Bank for environmental clean-up on the Northern border were redirected to bailing out Mexico's private banks.[106]

Caught in the Debt Trap

Chart Twelve

Distribution of Mexico's Foreign Debt end of 1995

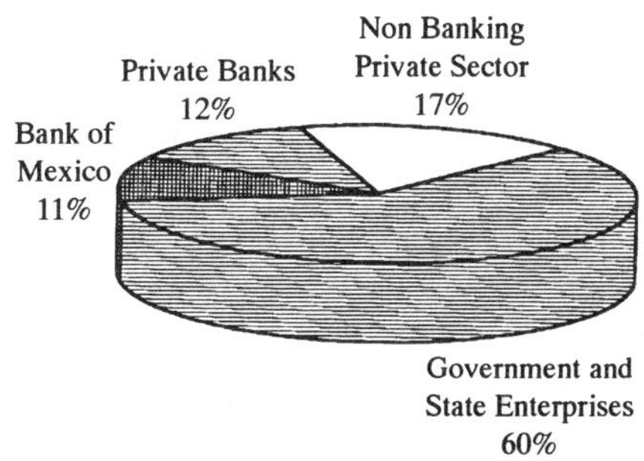

The Clinton rescue package only added more unpayable debts. Mexico is caught in a trap of having to borrow more to finance payments on old debts. The dramatic increase in Mexican debt for 1995, so evident in Chart Nine, reflects the effect of the rescue package. The rescue package involved replacing 85% of outstanding *tesobonos* with new bonds—that is, trading one kind of debt for another. Whereas the *tesobonos* were formerly accounted as internal government debt, even though most were held by foreigners, now they are counted as part of the Mexican government's external debt.

According to financial analysts ING Baring, the real interest rate paid by Mexico on its foreign debt in 1995 was 8.5%, significantly above market rates. The cost of debt service in 1996 will reach US$27.7 billion—$14 billion in interest and $13.7 billion in principal.

Payments of this magnitude are clearly unsustainable. These unsustainable debts may well prove to be the Achilles heel of speculative capitalism. Mexico's near default in 1982 threatened to bring down the global financial system. Crisis intervention saved the day. Once again in 1994 Mexico's financial troubles again threatened the whole system. Once again a huge rescue package was put together that served only to further increase the mountain of debt. Will the global financial system survive the next time?

How much does servicing the debt cost the people of Mexico?

The Mexican Action Network on Free Trade uses the following comparison to show how much debt payments cost. External debt servicing by Mexico during 1995 cost just about the same as all the following Mexican government programs put together:

the six principal anti-poverty programs - school breakfasts, tortilla subsidies, the special housing program, the rural road building program, the milk supply program and the special employment program;

the total budgets of four government departments - Health; Labour and Social Welfare; Environment, Natural Resources and Fishing; and Social Development; and the following social and cultural programs - pensions for around two million retirees; assistance to more than three million campesinos (peasant farmers) through the Direct Rural Assistance Program (PROCAMPO); support for university and postgraduate education; payment for 91,153 scholarships from the Public Education Department and the printing of 1,031,500 copies of publications for promoting culture; assistance for 13,928 athletes and support for the National Institute for Fine Arts and Literature.

Burdensome Conditions

The conditions attached to the Clinton/IMF rescue package are more far-reaching than any other set of structural adjustment conditions we have ever seen. The New York Times reported that the deal "effectively gives Washington veto power over much of Mexico's economic policy for the next decade."[107]

The structural adjustment measures involve deep cuts to government spending that ultimately harm economic recovery by reducing purchasing power in the domestic market. The tax system also became more regressive as the Value Added Tax, comparable to Canada's Goods and Services Tax, was raised from 10% to 15%.

The rescue package obliges Mexico to turn to the international financial market for new borrowing to roll over old debts. It requires further financial deregulation which can only benefit the speculators. It will even widen the scope for financial speculation through the privatization of the pension system. It requires a further deregulation and privatization of important industries such as petrochemicals, natural gas and electricity.

It obliges Pemex, the state oil company, to deposit oil export revenues in a New York bank, where they can be seized by the U.S. Federal Reserve Bank in the event that Mexico misses any debt payments.

This measure makes uninterrupted petroleum exports the key to financial solvency, an obligation that effectively nullifies one of the most significant exemptions that Mexico won during the NAFTA negotiations. The Mexican negotiators fought hard to protect Mexico's sovereignty over the quantity and pace of oil exports.

Unlike Canada, Mexico won an exemption from NAFTA's proportional sharing clause (Article 605), which obliges member countries to continue exporting non-renewable natural resources in the same proportion as they were exported over the previous three years, even in the event of domestic shortages. Now, for at least the next 10 years, Mexico has mortgaged its non-renewable hydrocarbons as collateral for foreign debt payments. This arrangement shows the power of finance capital to win a concession that the free trade negotiators could not obtain.

The rescue package also requires the further opening-up of Mexico's domestic financial system. Foreign banks are henceforth allowed to own 100% of Mexican banks. Among the first banks to take advantage of these new rules were the Bank of Montreal and the Bank of Nova Scotia, as we shall see below.

Mexico's Domestic Financial Sector

Mexico's extremely shaky domestic financial sector reveals another face of speculative capitalism. In Mexico the dominance of finance over production has reached its logical conclusion—bankruptcy for thousands of farmers and small businesses, who simply cannot make exorbitant interest payments and whose markets have disappeared due to the austerity imposed by foreign creditors. During the first 19 months after the peso devaluation, more than 15,800 small and medium-sized firms went bankrupt.[108]

During the external debt crisis of 1982, one of the last acts of outgoing President Lopez Portillo had been to nationalize the banks. Although he couched the manoeuvre under a flourish of revolutionary rhetoric, the international banks were in fact relieved. They hoped state control of the financial sector would enhance their chances of collecting on overdue loans.

As part of his neoliberal modernization program, Carlos Salinas reprivatized the banking system. Typically, Salinas used the bank privatization to bestow favours on his friends. At first glance, it looks like they paid a high price for the privilege of owning a bank—up to three times the assessed book value. But they were able to recover their investments rapidly by charging high interest rates and bank fees.

Immediately after the privatization, the spread between the interest rates Mexican banks collect on loans and what they pay on deposits began to rise. An international study found that, in September 1994, the spread between deposits and loans was 2.7 percentage points in the United States while it was 16.1 percentage points in Mexico.[109]

The reprivatized banks were so profitable that the new owners of the three major banks—Banamex, Bancomer and Banco Serfin—recovered all their investment in just two years. Instead of behaving like prudent, conservative lenders, the new bank owners pursued very loose (often irresponsible) lending policies. The Salinas government abetted this behaviour in 1989 by eliminating requirements that the banks keep reserves with the central bank, two years before the Mulroney government did the same thing in Canada.[110]

The number of personal loans and credit cards skyrocketed. It was not long before the incidence of non-performing loans was mounting and movements of bank debtors comprised of farmers, small business owners and credit card and mortgage holders sprang up all over the country. The largest and most famous of these grassroots movements is known as El Barzón.

El Barzón Mobilizes Debtors

El Barzón is a national network of small farmers, merchants, credit card owners and mortgage holders known for its militant actions against the banks. Barzonistas have tied up traffic with tractor demonstrations, occupied banks, burned credit cards and gone to jail for non-payment of loans despite Constitutional provisions that forbid jailing debtors.

The name, el Barzón, comes from a popular folk song dating from the 1910 Mexican Revolution. The song tells about the misery of landless farmers bound to the great haciendas. The Barzón refers to the strap that bound the plow to the horses or oxen or sometimes to the farmer.

Over 300,000 agricultural producers and small and medium business people participate in this grassroots movement in 30 states and the federal district. The Barzonistas protest the exorbitant interest rates charged by the banks, the high spread between rates paid on deposits and those charged on loans and the aggressive use of collection agencies to harass debtors and seize property for unpaid debts.

They do not refuse to pay all debts but instead say they will only pay what is just. Barzonistas have been critical of government bail-out programs because these have largely served to keep the banks afloat rather than treat the problems of debtors. In fact, one third of those who had their debts restructured under the government bail-out plans fell back into arrears.

While the Barzonistas want immediate debt relief and lower interest rates, they are aware that there is no solution to the debt problem without other measures to reactivate the economy. National Barzón leader Alfonso Ramirez Cuellar observes that even a total forgiveness of all outstanding debts would not solve the problem without a change in the neo-liberal economic policies of the Zedillo government.

Ramirez Cuellar recognizes that in order to solve Mexico's internal financial problems, the foreign debt, NAFTA, and the terms of the bailout accord with the Clinton administration must all be renegotiated. In particular the agricultural chapter of NAFTA must be changed to permit small farmers to survive. He also calls for the regulation of international finance. The Clinton rescue package must be changed because it insists that resources go to bailing out the banks instead of enabling the debtors to produce and earn enough to repay their loans.

Estimates of the extent of Mexico's domestic financial crisis vary. For example, the Department of Agriculture estimates that 150,734 farmers were in arrears on their payments in 1996, while El Barzón says the number is closer to 400,000.[111] According to the President of the National Bankers' Association, between December of 1994 and February 1996 the overdue loan portfolio increased by over 500%. In nominal terms, it went up to 120 billion new pesos, equivalent to 70% of total bank assets. Other estimates say that overdue loans were equivalent to 119% of bank assets in February of 1996.[112]

One problem that obscures the extent of the internal credit crisis is the fact that Mexican banks employ a less rigid definition of overdue loans than do banks in Canada and the United States. Under the Mexican system, a debtor has to miss three payments in a row before a loan is counted as non-performing. Under that system, 17% of outstanding loans were counted as overdue in December of 1995. When measured according to international accounting standards, non-performing loans were 23% of total outstanding credits.

Moreover, if the accounting criteria used in the U.S. (where missing one payment puts the loan in arrears) were employed, then the incidence of non-performing loans would be 34%.[113]

The Mexican Action Network on Free Trade puts this situation into perspective by recalling how Spain, in the heat of its financial crisis a decade ago, declared a state of emergency when 8% of a bank's outstanding credits were in arrears.[114]

Another Bail-out for the Rich

The Mexican government has announced seven different programs to rescue the financial sector. These include programs to purchase bad loans from the banks (transferring the risks to taxpayers); subsidies for interest rates; and the restructuring of loans.

So far, the Zedillo government has made 83,900 million pesos (US$10,896 million) available to support the financial system. Zedillo's bailout is costing the equivalent of more than 5% of GDP, or about 20 times as much as the amount spent on social programs for the poor. Like the

Clinton rescue plan, it is basically a bail-out for the rich. Low-income debtors benefit little from the plan.

The Zedillo government is financing the bail-out with US$1,750 million worth of credits from the World Bank and the Inter-American Development Bank. Yet it is still expected that additional resources will be needed.[115]

Ultimately, the financial rescue could cost US$20 billion, which is 50% more than the government received when it reprivatized the banks in 1991-92 (about US$13 billion). Not one bank, no matter how poorly managed, has been closed or taken over by the state. Financial analysts for the Weston group have observed that "This protection from failure provides managers with perverse incentives."[116]

Bank of Montreal and Bank of Nova Scotia Buy In

Given the precarious situation just described, why are several foreign banks, including two Canadian banks—the Bank of Montreal and the Bank of Nova Scotia—making investments in Mexican banks? Should not bankers' legendary prudence and conservative instincts make them wary of such high risks? Their haste to take a fling on the Mexican market reveals a lot about "risk-taking" in the new era of speculative capitalism.

In a revealing interview with the Mexican newsmagazine *Proceso*[117], a European banker spoke frankly on condition of anonymity about how international banks view Mexico. He acknowledges that Mexico's domestic financial sector is in much worse shape than the government or the banks or the international financial institutions would ever concede publicly. He then says that the problems are so serious that the Mexican authorities are scrambling to cover up the most serious breaches while they look for international financial groups to take over the banks and clean up the mess.

He explains that a complete cleanup would involve writing off masses of unrecoverable loans, recapitalizing the banks with foreign money, modernizing their management and information technologies, reducing their personnel, and integrating them totally with the international operations of larger banks.

To make this operation feasible, the Mexican banks are being offered for sale at rock bottom prices. Accordingly, the Bank of Montreal and the Bank of Nova Scotia paid very little for the assets they acquired. The Bank of Montreal paid US$456 million for a 16% share in Bancomer. But $440 million of that is in Brady bonds it has held since 1990.

The Bank of Montreal is gambling that it will make a higher return from its ownership stake in Bancomer than it would by holding onto its Brady Bonds. As one of its executives told _Toronto Star_ reporter Linda Diebel, "If Mexico defaulted tomorrow, the bank would only get about 30 cents to the dollar on immediate redemption of those bonds."[118] So why not take advantage of the fact that the Mexican government desperately wants to keep Bancomer afloat?

The Bank of Montreal had already received tax write-offs from Canadian taxpayers when it converted its former Mexican debt to Brady Bonds in 1990. Now it is getting set to cash in on subsidies from Mexican taxpayers.

The Bank of Nova Scotia's US$225 million investment for a 55% ownership of Banco Inverlat will also benefit from Mexican government largesse. The Inverlat bank has been split into two divisions. The Bank of Nova Scotia will share in the ownership of the so-called "good" division, while the Mexican government is taking over most of the "bad" loans on Inverlat's books. Until the deal finally closes on March 31, 2000, it is up to the Mexican government "to satisfy all (Inverlat's) regulatory capital requirements."[119]

The European banker interviewed by _Proceso_ explains that most foreign banks are only looking to Mexico for short-term profits. They see a generalized economic crisis and all the ingredients for a very serious social crisis leading to continued political instability. Therefore, most banks are investing only in short-term financial instruments or taking minority shares in Mexican banks. (The Bank of Nova Scotia appears to be the exception.)

When asked why banks would still invest in a country undergoing severe economic, political and social turmoil, where there is a risk of total financial collapse, the European banker reveals the cynicism of the banking industry: "When a financier lends money or invests capital, his problem is not to loan to someone or invest in an industry that will not go bankrupt. Potentially, everyone can go broke. **His problem is to lend or invest up to 15 minutes before the crash**...[and then] get out on time."[120]

The Mexican Action Network on Free Trade speaks for many ordinary Mexicans when it expresses the resentment felt towards "Foreign banks [who] are taking advantage of the crisis to enter our market on very advantageous terms, not only by buying shares at bargain prices, but also by benefiting from the prevailing monopoly interest rates. Foreign banks are now receiving half of the profits generated by the system. They are beginning to surpass the limits for individual and market shares agreed upon in NAFTA."[121]

Basic Contradictions

Both the Clinton/IMF bail-out of Mexico's external debt and the Zedillo government's rescue of the domestic banking sector embody the same contradictions. Both rescue efforts aim to save the financial sector at the expense of the productive sector and social development. As we have shown in our book *Recolonization or Liberation*, orthodox Structural Adjustment Programs put the interests of financial creditors ahead of the basic need of the populations of indebted countries.

The same fundamental flaw exists in Zedillo's domestic financial rescue plan: "It is dependent on a resumption of economic growth in order to recover non-performing loans, but the exorbitant cost of protecting the banks will in fact stifle growth."[122]

As Alberto Arroyo points out so clearly, there is no solution to the problem of non-performing loans unless the external debt and NAFTA are renegotiated. Only then can domestic Mexican interest rates be lowered, since they will no longer have to remain high to attract foreign capital.[123] There can be no solution to the internal financial crisis without reactivation of investment in production.

Alberto Arroyo argues that, instead of using public funds collected through taxation to save the private banks from bankruptcy, the same resources must be used to promote economic growth so that the productive sector may recover and pay its own way.[124]

CHAPTER FIVE

Capital Must be Regulated

"Loose funds may sweep around the world, disorganizing all steady business. Nothing is more certain than that movement of capital funds must be regulated."

—John Maynard Keynes, 1941

The international financial system may be compared to a huge body of water. Viewed from afar it appears calm, like the ocean photographed from outer space. It seems to be an efficient way of allocating resources from areas of surplus to regions in deficit. However, the closer one gets to the sea, the more evident are the waves, swells, tides, eddies and whirlpools that crash and slosh about.

In this study, we have examined how a growing tide of speculation has detached finance from production. As markets are deregulated, the seas become more unpredictable. As The Economist put it, "Just as the new international dimension of finance has added to some risks that may help to start a crisis... it has weakened the traditional remedies of economic policy. In the new world of finance, the seas are rougher and the life-rafts flimsier."[125]

Indeed, today's rough financial seas are more like the turbulent periods of the 19th and early 20th centuries. A series of international lending booms and busts over the years 1808-10, 1823-25, 1856-61, 1885-90, 1910-13 and 1924-28 all ended with borrowers defaulting on their obligations. Sometimes payments were resumed during the next upswing, but usually the creditors suffered huge losses.[126]

What is unique about this century is the relative stability of the post-World War II period from 1946 though to 1970. Part of the reason for this stability was the Bretton Woods system, based on a strong U.S. dollar said to be "as good as gold."

Domestic financial regulation also played an important role. After the trauma of the Great Depression, national governments brought greater stability to financial markets through banking regulations, reserve requirements, deposit insurance, limits on interest rates, and the separation of commercial banking (taking deposits and making loans) from investment banking (underwriting issues of stocks and bonds).

A large part of today's problem is that both the Bretton Woods system and the national regulation of finance capital have broken down. Some commentators argue that deregulation was inevitable because of unstoppable technological change and market pressures. For example, *The Economist* maintains that deregulation is "often no more than an acknowledgment that the rules are no longer working."[127] They argue that governments have had to loosen national regulations in response to the tactics of private financial institutions who shifted their operations to other less regulated jurisdictions.

In an essay on "Democratic Governance in an Era of Global Finance," economic historian Eric Helleiner disputes this contention: "Although technological and market developments have been important, states have themselves actively encouraged the globalization process... particularly [through] decisions to liberalize capital controls."[128]

Helleiner shows how governments had a variety of motives for pursuing deregulation. Some saw short-term gains from opening up their domestic financial sectors to inflows of footloose capital. All were lobbied by politically powerful financial corporations who wanted to enjoy the same freedoms as their competitors in other jurisdictions.

Some governments, such as the Thatcher, Reagan and Mulroney administrations, identified with the neoliberal ideas of Friedrich Hayek and Milton Friedman. These neoliberals argued that governments should leave monetary and financial affairs up to market forces. According to this ideology, "the elimination of capital controls not only encourages a more efficient allocation of capital and removes a set of restrictions on individual liberty; it also ensures that democratic governments are appropriately disciplined by international financial markets when they attempt to pursue policies in the macroeconomic, tax and regulatory realms that undermine the vitality and freedoms of a market economy."[129]

In their essay "In Defense of Capital Controls," James Crotty and Gerald Epstein argue persuasively that capital movements can still be controlled by national governments. The decision not to control capital movements is political, not an inevitable consequence of new technology or market forces. However, these new circumstances do make the challenge a formidable one.

All of the reforms discussed in this chapter have the same ultimate goal—the restoration of democratic control over financial flows. Democratic control over finance is not an end in itself. It is, however, a necessary prerequisite for building a more just and environmentally sustainable economy, for creating jobs, and for reducing inequality.

Capital controls are necessary to defuse the threat of capital flight which hobbles democratic governance. Without them, unelected, wealthy financiers acquire a veto over political and economic decisions. "The markets vote every day," says multi-billionaire financier George Soros. "They force governments to adopt unpopular but indispensable measures."[130]

Revisiting Bretton Woods

In Chapter Two of _Debt Bondage or Self-Reliance,_ we explain the background to the 1944 Bretton Woods conference which established the International Monetary Fund (IMF) and the World Bank. There we explain why many of John Maynard Keynes's original proposals for a post-war monetary system were set aside or modified.

At Bretton Woods, the decisive factor was not the intellectual merits of Keynes's ideas, but the reality of U.S. power.[131] As the holder of most of Britain's war debts, the U.S. was able to use its leverage to dictate most of the terms.

In the preparatory stage before Bretton Woods, both Keynes, representing England, and the chief U.S. delegate, Harry Dexter White, agreed on one fundamental point—that controls on international capital movements are essential to allow national governments to pursue full employment policies. In an early draft of proposals for Bretton Woods, White even suggested that governments not allow deposits or investments from another country without the approval of that country's government.[132]

When the New York bankers got wind of this, they put pressure on the U.S. Treasurer, Henry Morgenthau, to instruct White to modify his draft. Nevertheless, the final Bretton Woods arrangements did allow national governments to control capital flows in and out of their national economies.

In *Debt Bondage,* we review the reasons why the Bretton Woods system broke down as more U.S. dollars were held abroad than could be redeemed for gold stored at Fort Knox. When President Nixon went on television on August 15, 1971, and unilaterally announced that the U.S. dollar would no longer be redeemable for gold, he was trying to stem a wave of speculation against the greenback. In fact, Nixon's speech marked the end of the Bretton Woods era and the beginning of the new era of speculative capitalism.

After the collapse of the Bretton Woods system, the Eurocurrency market began to grow by leaps and bounds. Eurocurrencies are moneys deposited outside the issuing country, for example U.S. dollars deposited in Swiss banks or German marks held in Britain. In 1971, the pool of Eurocurrency deposits was worth about US$150 billion. By 1983, it had reached over US$2.2 trillion. Now the Bank for International Settlements estimates that the pool of hot money that sloshes about the globe is worth over US$13 trillion.

What is significant is not only the amounts involved, but the fact that all this internationally held money is unregulated. Banks are free to create new money through Eurocurrency loans without any reserve requirements. There is no world central bank to act as lender of last resort, as there is in a national banking system.

The most that can be done is that the Bank for International Settlements can try to co-ordinate actions by its members, the central banks of the largest industrial countries. But, as we saw in Chapter Two, these national central banks are relatively weak in the face of the huge pools of private capital that wash around the globe.

Eleven Crises Since 1973

According to the IMF, there have been 11 significant crises since 1973 that required co-ordinated international crisis management by monetary authorities. Each of these crises was contained chiefly through the issue of new credit, not by addressing the fundamental underlying causes. Susan Strange of the London School of Economics notes that the IMF, governments and central banks have been adept at dealing with the crises, "while the chronic problems have always been dodged and avoided."[133]

The most recent of these crises is the Mexican peso crisis examined in Chapter Four. The managing director of the IMF, Michel Camdessus, calls Mexico "the first crisis of the 21st century".[134] Two factors make this crisis different from the Mexican debt crisis of 1982. First, there is the role of speculative, fly-by-night capital. The second factor is the size of the rescue package. Our analysis in Chapter Four shows how the new lending has only deepened Mexico's underlying debt problems by adding to the mountain of unpayable debt.

The questions we must face are: Can we go on lurching from crisis to crisis? Will the issue of new credit suffice the next time a major country, like Mexico, cannot meet its obligations? The unregulated flows of finance analyzed in this report make future crises inevitable. Can we recall the lessons learned after the Great Depression that financial markets must be regulated and that the international movement of money must be controlled?

One danger of bail-outs, like the Clinton/IMF rescue of investors in Mexican bonds, is that the speculators will now take on even greater risks because they expect yet another bail-out if serious trouble recurs. They may think that some countries, or some banks, or some financial markets, are simply too big to be allowed to fail.

As David Felix comments, "The successive government bail-outs of international financial markets from the crises to which they have become increasingly prone have [raised] moral hazard risks, encouraging yet greater speculative flows. This increases the prospect that future crises may exceed the fire-fighting capability of the G-7 monetary authorities... The likelihood of a future crisis exceeding the crisis management resources of the befuddled monetary authorities is becoming uncomfortably high."[136]

Even if the world's financial elite does not lead us onto the shoals, the global financial order must be reformed in order to allow us to make social and political choices that redress the growing inequality we highlighted in Chapter One.

How can we bring finance under control? The answers to this question are many and varied. Given the scope of the problem, there is no one simple solution. In the balance of this chapter we shall discuss 13 possible courses of action. We begin with the most ambitious proposals for restoring control over financial capital. Next we discuss some immediate measures that could be taken at the national level to rein in speculation. Finally, we point to some practical measures that can be taken at a local community level to regain democratic control over finance.

A. REGULATING FINANCE CAPITAL

Financial regulation is needed at both the national and international levels. National controls alone won't suffice, because so much of the explosive growth of credit occurs in the Euromarkets that operate in what A. Smith calls "a wonderful country called Offshore... where there [are] no rules at all because there [is no world government.]"[137]

1. A New United Nations Conference on Money and Finance

In the past, we in ECEJ have called on the Canadian government to sponsor preparatory work for a new United Nations Conference on Money and Finance. This conference would aim to recreate a stable world monetary system. It would have to involve more participants than the original Bretton Woods Conference, in keeping with the growth in United Nations membership over its 50-year history.

The purpose of such a conference would be to recapture for our times John Maynard Keynes's vision of a world order that would counteract the current global increase in misery and mass unemployment and, in Canada, prevent a return to conditions of the 1930s. To achieve this goal, Keynes believed that national governments had to have enough control over international capital flows to enable them to pursue policies of full employment and social justice.

In our day, such a conference would also have to ratify plans for significant debt relief for less developed countries. These debts must be written down, not only because of the unacceptably high costs their payment imposes on the people of the Third World. They must also be reduced to lessen the threat of further financial crises that imperil the well-being of all the world's citizens.

The history of the original 1944 Bretton Woods Conference shows that preparatory work is crucial for the success of such an endeavour. One starting point for the design of a new financial system is to revisit the original ideas Keynes prepared in anticipation of the Bretton Woods conference.

Professor Hans W. Singer[138] explains the basic features of Keynes's original design:

- a world central bank, which he called a "Clearing Union", which would extend credit to countries with balance of payments deficits and hold deposits from countries with balance of payments surpluses;
- an international currency, which he dubbed the "Bancor," although he thought a better name could be found, as the unit for international transactions;
- an International Trade Organization, which among other things would have stabilized commodity prices through buffer stocks and commodity agreements; and
- an aid program linked directly to the United Nations which would provide low-cost loans and grants to less developed countries without the kind of conditions that were subsequently attached to IMF and World Bank loans.

Unfortunately, none of these ideas was ever implemented in its original form. The institutions that emerged from the actual Bretton Woods conference were very different. In direct opposition to Keynes's views, the IMF began to impose stiff austerity measures on countries with balance of payments deficits.

Keynes had wanted the Clearing Union to finance these deficits in the interest of growth and full employment, while imposing penalties on countries that ran large surpluses. The International Trade Organization (ITO) never got off the ground because the U.S. Congress refused to ratify the Havana Charter. Instead of a comprehensive ITO, the world was left with only a very inadequate substitute, the General Agreement on Tariffs and Trade (GATT).

Of course, Keynes's ideas would have to be modified to meet the particular requirements of our era. In addition to the core functions outlined above, the new United Nations monetary authority would have to play a major role in writing down less developed countries' debts. Some means would also have to be found for dealing with the existing pools of international hot money.

Here we have no easy answers, only suggestions to be debated and refined. Korten suggests that the new UN body would establish reserve requirements for quasi-international currencies like Eurodollars.[139] Schor and Epstein suggest a "substitution account" to allow governments to convert Eurodollars into the new international currency.[140] Wachtel advocates a "public debt authority" that would reschedule international debts purchased from creditors at a discount.[141]

2. The Tobin Tax

The construction of a whole new international financial system is a huge challenge that will take many years to achieve. What can be done in the interim to at least begin to cool down hot money?

The best alternative we have would be to negotiate an international agreement to institute a small tax on international financial transactions. This proposal is known as "the Tobin Tax," after its designer, Nobel prize-winning economist James Tobin. Tobin himself points out that a transaction tax would be a second best alternative to having a truly international currency. Nevertheless, in the short run it may be the best and most feasible alternative.

The basic idea of the Tobin Tax is simple. It would involve a modest tax of between 0.1% and 0.25% on all foreign exchange transactions. The tax would discourage short-term speculation without interfering with trade or long-term productive investments. David Felix likens the Tobin Tax to "sin taxes" on alcohol or tobacco, which "penalize and thus restrict socially undesirable behaviour."[142]

A Tobin Tax would restrict short-term speculation more than long-term investment, because the shorter the term the steeper the tax. The following table presents several examples of the different effect of a 0.25% Tobin Tax on investments held for different time periods. All the examples assume the purchase and resale of a one-million-dollar bond. Since the Tobin Tax would be applied on the full value of the transaction each time it leaves or enters a country, its effect is doubled for a two-way round trip. What makes each example different is the time frame.

As can readily be seen from the table, the effective annual tax rate is highest for short-term currency speculation. The 120% annualized rate cited here is for illustrative purposes. In reality, no one would make the same trade every day. What the table does show is that, for an overnight round trip into and out of another currency to be profitable, the change in the value of the currency would have to be greater than 0.5%. For a one-way trade, the margin of difference would have to exceed the tax rate—that is, 0.25%—to make the trade worthwhile.

Since many speculative currency trades occur on much smaller margins of difference, the Tobin Tax would indeed be an effective deterrent.

Table Five

Effect of a 0.25% Tobin Tax on $1Million Round Trip

type of financial instrument	tax per period	effective annual tax rate	how annual tax rate is calculated
10 year bond	$5,000 over 10 years or $500 a year	0.05%	0.25% X 2 trips divided by 10 years
1 year bond	$5,000 a year	0.5%	0.25% X 2 trips X 1 year
90 day bond	$5,000 every 3 months	2%	0.25X X 2 trips X 4 quarters
30 day bond	$5,000 a month	6%	0.25% X 2 trips X 12 months
overnight currency speculation	$5,000 a day	120%	0.25% X 2 trips X 240 business days

James Tobin maintains that the most important effect of his proposed tax may not be its deterrence of currency speculation, but rather the leeway it would give for autonomous national monetary policies.[143] As the box shows, a 0.25% transaction tax would allow Canada to maintain up to a two-percentage-point differential on three-month interest rates.

How a Tobin Tax Would Allow a Wider Interest Rate Spread

A transactions tax on foreign exchange transactions could help give the Bank of Canada more room to manoeuvre. Let's consider a simplified example involving the effect of a 0.25% Tobin tax on interest rates on three-month Treasury bills. Remember that interest rates are always quoted in annual terms even when they apply to bonds that mature every three months, that is every quarter. When three-month bonds mature the holder collects interest worth one quarter of the annual rate.

Consider a speculator holding a $1,000 three-month Canadian bond with a nominal interest rate of 8%. At the end of three months that bond would pay (1,000 X (8/4=2)%=20) $20 worth of interest. Now suppose the speculator notices that US short-term rates have climbed to 10%. He or she would be tempted to sell the Canadian bond and buy the US Treasury Bill. At the end of three months the US Bill would yield (1,000 X (10/4=2.5)%=25) $25 in interest, five dollars more than the Canadian bond.

Assuming that the trader wants to bring the money back to Canada again as soon as the US bond matures, he or she would face a 0.25% transaction tax charged on the full amount each time the money crossed the border. Therefore the total cost of the tax (1,000 X 0.25% = 2.50 X 2) $5.00 would cancel out the five dollar potential gain. In theory the leeway afforded to the Bank of Canada to set short-term interest rates would be two percentage points. In practice the effect of the tax would be diminished by the fact that many investors would make only a one-way trade, keeping their money outside the country until Canadian rates improved.

Support for a Tobin Tax is growing, particularly among groups concerned with international development. Thanks to the efforts of the United Nations Development Program which sponsored a volume of essays entitled The Tobin Tax: Coping with Financial Volatility, the idea is now being taken seriously by monetary economists.[144] Even the skeptics concede that the tax would be effective in slowing down speculation.

There appears to be an emerging consensus that the tax would have to be somewhat smaller than the 0.5% that Tobin originally proposed. Tobin himself now says the tax should be no higher than 0.25%, and perhaps as low as 0.1%.[145] However, debate continues on how best to design such a tax, on who should administer it, and on how to guard against tax avoidance.

It is frequently argued that a Tobin Tax would fail because speculators would use offshore tax havens to avoid the tax. David Felix effectively counters this argument by pointing out that nearly 80% of all short-term foreign exchange transactions in 1992 were handled in just seven countries—the United Kingdom, the United States, Japan, Singapore, Switzerland, Hong Kong and Germany.

Felix argues that a uniform tax applied by these seven countries would cover most transactions. Furthermore, "large trading institutions are not likely to risk [their] reputation in order to evade a small tax. They can be expected to push against the legal limits through financial innovating, but not blatantly violate them."[146]

Peter Kenen persuasively argues that collecting the tax at the dealing site and charging a high punitive tax rate on trades with tax havens would effectively prevent the migration of trading to tax havens.[147]

To the extent a Tobin Tax lowers the volume of foreign exchange transactions, it becomes easier for central banks to intervene in foreign exchange markets. For example, the decline in speculation that might be expected to result from a 0.25% Tobin Tax could raise the ratio of official central bank reserves to foreign exchange volume by as much as 30%.[148] The central banks would have a double advantage if they themselves were exempt from having to pay the tax, as David Felix and Ranjit Sau suggest.[149]

Estimates of the revenue potential of a Tobin Tax vary according to the assumptions made. A realistic set of estimates by David Felix and

Ranjit Sau put the global revenue potential at around US$302 billion a year for a 0.25% tax; US$148 billion for a 0.1% tax; and US$90 billion at a 0.05% tax rate.[150] According to the same source, the Canadian share of global tax revenues would amount to US$5.5 billion for a 0.25% tax; US$2.6 billion for a 0.1% tax; and US$1.6 billion for a 0.05% tax. These calculations assume 1995 foreign exchange volumes, pre-tax transition costs of 0.5%, and the non-taxation of 35% of foreign exchange trading due to the exemption of official transactions (10%) and tax evasion (25%).

There is considerable debate concerning how these tax revenues should be used. Ideally, most of the revenue from an international tax should be used to fund international bodies such as the United Nations. Many people involved in international development look to a Tobin Tax to fund genuine economic and social development initiatives in the Third World through United Nations agencies.

For example, the World Summit on Social Development, held in Copenhagen in 1995, estimated that a world poverty eradication program would require US$40 billion a year, in addition to what is presently available for foreign aid. The 1992 UN Conference on Environment and Development in Rio de Janeiro estimated that about US$125 billion a year is needed to tackle environmental challenges.[151]

Pragmatists argue that, in order to make the Tobin Tax more attractive, a considerable portion of the revenue should remain in the hands of the national governments that collect it. For example, Inge Kaul and John Langmore suggest a formula whereby low-income and middle-income less-developed countries would retain 100% of the proceeds; higher-income developing countries would retain 90% of the proceeds, and high-income countries 80% of the amount they collect. They calculate that a 0.1% Tobin Tax distributed this way would leave about US$27 billion a year available for international purposes.[152]

In our view, we should aim for a higher proportion of the tax to be available for international purposes ranging from peacekeeping to social development to environmental protection. Of course, the ultimate disposition of the tax would have to be determined by an international treaty negotiated under United Nations auspices. A good case can certainly be made for allowing low-income less-developed countries to keep 100% of the revenue they collect, since relatively little foreign exchange is traded within their jurisdictions.

A redistributive formula would have to be negotiated so that the money-centres are neither unduly penalized, causing them to refrain from participating, nor unduly rewarded by an international tax.

3. A Domestic Financial Transactions Tax (FTT)

The original inspiration for the Tobin Tax actually came from another of John Maynard Keynes's ideas, which he applied to the domestic rather than the international economy. Reflecting on the excessive speculation occurring in the United States in the 1930s, Keynes wrote: "It is usually agreed that casinos should in the public interest be inaccessible and expensive. And perhaps the same is true of stock exchanges...The introduction of a substantial government transfer tax on all transactions might prove the most serviceable reform available, with a view to mitigating the predominance of speculation over enterprise."[153]

In fact, many countries already have some form of domestic financial transaction tax. Australia, Austria, Belgium, Finland, France, Germany, Hong Kong, Italy, Japan, Singapore, Sweden, and the United Kingdom already have taxes on the sale of stocks or bonds.[154] Canada is one of the few industrialized countries that do not have excise taxes on the transfer of financial securities. Even the United States has a small 0.0033% Security and Exchange Commission fee charged on stock sales.[155]

A domestic Financial Transfer Tax (FTT) would have the same goal as the Tobin Tax—to deter speculation. An FTT as low as 0.1% on bond sales would deter much speculation, since nowadays in Canada speculators buy and sell bonds to take advantage of interest rate margins as low as 0.03% to 0.1%.

Moreover, an FTT would be a progressive measure, since the wealthy use the banking system more than low-income people. The revenue potential of an FTT depends on the scope of financial services covered. Some proponents say that it should be universal, covering all cheques, withdrawals, transfers or other debits from any financial institution. Accountant Jack Biddell estimates that, since about $27 trillion is cleared annually by Canada's banking system, a 0.1% FTT would raise about $27 billion in revenue every year. By contrast, the Goods and Services Tax raised about $17.4 billion in 1995.

Alternatively, an FTT might be applied only to certain kinds of financial transactions. If a 0.1% tax were applied only to stocks, bonds and money market trades in Canada, it would yield $3.5 billion at 1993 trading volumes.[156] This estimate excludes ordinary bank transactions by individuals. It also excludes options, futures, and derivative contracts, which certainly should be taxed.

Another advantage of an FTT is its simplicity. It could be programmed into bank computers and deducted automatically, just as bank fees are now.

One of the main arguments against a universal FTT concerns the difficulty of preventing it from applying to the same end product several times (the cascading effect). This is not a new problem for Canadian tax authorities. The old Manufacturers' Sales Tax, which was replaced by the GST, confronted the same difficulty. Accounting procedures would have to be developed to avoid double taxation. For example, businesses might receive a tax credit equal to the FTT rate times their income-tax-deductible expenses.[157]

Another argument is that an FTT might cause more people to take their money offshore. The key to avoiding this would be to make sure that an FTT apply to all Canadian residents and their affiliated companies, regardless of where the transactions take place. An FTT would also apply to the Canadian transactions of non-residents.

The flight of capital abroad can also be slowed down through special withholding taxes that apply only to transactions that cross national borders.

Non-resident speculators often borrow a country's currency from a financial institution for later resale. To reduce such speculation, countries could place a special tax on lending to non-residents or require that a portion of such loans be put into a non-interest bearing account.

An FTT could also have a variable rate, depending on the duration of the period for which a financial instrument is held, or be applied only to short-term speculative transactions. For example, the resale of a financial instrument held for less than one or two years could be taxed at a higher rate than an instrument held for a longer term.

International speculation could be deterred by taxing gains from cross-border investments at a higher rate.

4. International Cooperation to Lower Interest Rates

Much of the international flow of hot money analyzed in this study occurs because speculators are constantly seeking marginally higher returns on their investments. As Howard Wachtel explains, "The comparative rate of interest paid in one country versus another is... the major indicator used by speculators to decide where to put their cash on any given day and during any particular hour of the day."[158]

Countries wanting to attract capital will offer slightly higher interest rates than their neighbours. A country wishing to lower its domestic interest rates will hesitate to do so lest the result be a wave of capital flight. The result is a perverse ratchet effect whereby central banks can always raise rates but have difficulty lowering them.

To deal with this problem, Wachtel calls for international cooperation among central banks "to remove the speculative bulge in interest rates [which would be like] the twice yearly resetting of our clocks [for daylight saving time]."[159] The central banks of the most powerful financial trading nations would have to coordinate their efforts to gradually bring down interest rates.

5. Debt Relief for Less Developed Countries

The Third World debt crisis burst onto the public agenda in August of 1982 when Mexico announced it could not make its debt payments. That year, total less-developed-country debt equalled US$850 billion. Over the ensuing 12 years, 1983-1994, Third World countries transferred about US$2 trillion to Northern creditors in interest and principal payments.

Despite this enormous displacement of wealth from the South to the North, by the end of 1994 the total debt had risen to US$1.95 trillion.[160] While new loans accounted for part of the increase, a major reason why the total rose was that unpaid interest was rolled over into new credits.

Despite the minor debt relief that has occurred for some private bank debt under the Brady Plan and for some government-to-government loans, less-developed countries are still transferring some US$100 billion worth of debt payments to the North every year.[161]

Such high payments are simply unsustainable. In calling for debt relief, our first concern is for the well-being of the peoples who endure hunger and privation as scarce resources are channeled away from economic and social development.

We must also realize, however, that the peoples of the North have reasons to want these debts written down. Susan George calls the many ways that Southern debt impacts on the North the "debt boomerangs".[162] One boomerang is environmental as the debtors' desperate efforts to earn foreign exchange is leading to deforestation and resulting in global warming and the loss of biological diversity.

Another boomerang is the growth of the illicit drug trade as Southern governments, desperate for investment, turn a blind eye to the drug trade or take bribes from the drug lords.

A third boomerang is the cost of bailing out creditors with public money in the absence of programs that make the speculators bear the consequences of their actions.

The fourth boomerang is the loss of jobs in the North as Southern markets are stifled by Structural Adjustment Programs.

A fifth boomerang is the cost of dealing with rising crime and conflicts that break out in the Third World.

The debt crisis is particularly acute for 30 severely indebted low-income countries (SILICs), 25 of which are located in sub-Sahara Africa. In 1982, the total debt of the SILICs was equivalent to about one-third of their Gross National Product (GNP) and twice as big as their export earnings. By 1992, SILICs debts were 120% as large as their total GNP and five times as large as their export earnings. Since these countries cannot qualify for many commercial loans, most of their debts are owed to governments and to the multilateral financial institutions like the World Bank, the IMF, and the regional development banks.

In August 1995, the Mexican Action Network on Free Trade, along with 14 other civic organizations, convened an important meeting on Foreign Debt and Alternatives. We in the Ecumenical Coalition for Economic Justice participated, along with representatives of civil society from five continents. The following discussion builds on the specific proposals that emerged from that forum.[163]

For bilateral government-to-government debt, a starting point for action is what is known as the "Naples terms" endorsed by the heads of the Group of Seven (G7) governments at their Naples Summit in 1994. The Naples terms call for 50% to 67% reductions of principal on governmental loans. As of mid-1995, only one country—Uganda—had achieved a 67% reduction of its debts.

Even if the full 67% discount were applied, it would not be sufficient. A simulation by the World Bank found that 20 of 33 SILICs would still face unsustainable debts. A more realistic simulation by the European Network on Debt and Development (EURODAD), a non-governmental organization, found that only one of the 33 countries could pay its debts if the Naples terms were applied.

The groups participating in the International Meeting on External Debt and Alternatives therefore agreed that we must strive for deeper debt reduction than the Group of Seven had to offer. In September 1996, the governments participating in the "Paris Club" of government creditors agreed to relieve up to 80% of the bilateral debts owed by the SILICs.

This new offer does not include new debts incurred after a country first applied for relief, nor debts owed for official development assistance. The 1996 announcement was part of a wider debt relief package involving multilateral creditors, particularly the World Bank and the International Monetary Fund (IMF).

World Bank officials say the 80% level of relief still is not enough to reduce the debt burden for some countries to sustainable levels.[164] The World Bank and the IMF had wanted the Paris Club to offer up to 90% relief on bilateral debts. However, their advocacy is not entirely disinterested. If the Paris Club were to offer 90% instead of 80% debt relief, then the cost to the World Bank and the IMF and the regional development banks of an integrated debt relief package for 20 SILICs would be lower.[165]

While the September 1996 decision by the World Bank to offer some debt relief sets a precedent, it does not adequately address the enormity of the debt problem. While the proportion of the total debt of the SILICs owed to the multilateral banks is relatively small (about 20%), 48% of their actual debt service payments flow to these institutions. SILIC debt service obligations to multilateral institutions rose almost five-fold between 1982 and 1994, from just under US$8.5 billion to almost US$40 billion.

Moreover, the issue of how to pay for this debt relief is not yet resolved. The World Bank will fund its US$1.9 billion contribution from its substantial net income. There is not yet agreement on a British initiative to sell a portion of the IMF's US$40 billion gold stockpile to finance debt relief. Germany adamantly opposes sale of IMF gold. For the time being, the IMF will finance its US$1.2 billion participation from its own reserves. The issue of selling off a portion of the IMF's gold reserves has been postponed.

The biggest problem with the multilateral debt relief initiative is that, in order to be eligible, debtor countries must have a proven track record of successfully implementing Structural Adjustment Programs (SAPs) for up to six years. Moreover, instead of offering outright debt relief, the IMF is manoeuvring to use the crisis in multilateral debt as an excuse to expand its Enhanced Structural Adjustment Facility (ESAF).[166] The managing director of the IMF, Michel Camdessus, initially rejected the idea of selling off some IMF gold. However, he has since embraced the idea as a way of making the ESAF permanent.[167]

In our book *Recolonization or Liberation*, we analyze in detail why orthodox SAPs have failed to meet their stated goals of promoting investment and growth, reducing debts and improving incomes. In that study we show that the one group that has benefited from SAPs consists of the financiers. If debt relief is to succeed, it is essential that the kinds of conditions typically demanded by the IMF and World Bank be replaced with new policies like those in the African Alternative Framework to Structural Adjustment Programs for Socio-Economic Recovery and Transformation (AAF).

Although the AAF was published by the UN Economic Commission for Africa in 1989 and endorsed by the heads of African governments, its implementation has been stymied by the requirements of debt payments and SAPs imposed from without.

Strict adherence to orthodox SAPs, and to the neoliberal policies which accompany them have failed to alleviate poverty or promote true economic development in sub-Saharan Africa, Latin America, and the poorest nations of Asia. In fact, they have led to a deepening chasm between the wealthy and the poor, and have often fomented social unrest and violence. It is time to try other measures, such as the alternatives outlined in the Mexican Citizens' "Liberty Referendum"[168] and the African Alternative Framework.[169] It would be a great tragedy if debt relief served only to make less-developed countries' payments more sustainable without allowing them to escape from the debt trap because strict Structural Adjustment Programs were imposed as conditions for eligibility.

As the Mexican case study shows, strict adherence to SAPs is a recipe for continued stagnation, not economic recovery.

For the larger, higher-income debtor countries, money owed to mutual funds has overtaken private bank debt as the principal problem. An important precedent was set with the 1989 Brady Plan, which established the principle that private bank debts owed by Third World countries could indeed be written down. As we saw in Chapter Four, the problem was that the amount of debt relief offered under the Brady Plan was insufficient.

Participants in the Mexico City conference agreed that the same kind of debt relief must be negotiated for the current debts owed to mutual funds. We rejected the argument that these debts cannot be renegotiated because they are widely dispersed. The same was true of bank debts in the 1980s, as numerous small banks held portions of larger loans arranged by the leading money-centre banks. Nevertheless, renegotiations took place under the leadership of the largest banks.

In the case of the mutual funds, similar consortia could be formed to negotiate orderly write-downs of what are ultimately uncollectable debts.

As the prospects for new Official Development Assistance to less-developed countries diminish, the best way to augment funds for social and economic development would be through a Tobin Tax. These revenues should be dedicated to sustainable economic and social development under United Nations auspices.

In many ways, a United Nations fund financed by the Tobin Tax would constitute the fourth pillar of the world order envisioned by Keynes prior to Bretton Woods. Keynes's vision of an independent fund for less-developed countries never materialized, because the World Bank took over the soft loan International Development Association, which originally was supposed to be administered by the United Nations.[170]

6. Renegotiate NAFTA

The Mexican experience also shows the need to renegotiate international treaties such as the North American Free Trade Agreement (NAFTA), which prevent countries from controlling speculative capital flows. Some of the specific changes that should be made to NAFTA include:

a) **changes to the investment chapter to permit governments to require foreign investment to be used for productive purposes instead of speculation.** This would involve removing the restrictions on performance requirements in NAFTA Article 1106 which prevent governments from requiring that foreign investors purchase inputs locally or employ their citizens.

b) **changes to the energy chapter to restore national sovereignty over the exploitation of renewable and non-renewable natural resources.** This would require removing Articles 315 and 604, which prohibit Canada from restricting the level of exports of non-renewable resources to less than the amount exported over the previous three years. As we saw in Chapter Four, Mexico won an exception to this rule, but that exemption has been effectively overruled by the terms of the Clinton bail-out for the financial sector.

c) **revision of NAFTA Articles 1109 and 1401:2 which forbid all kinds of capital and foreign exchange controls.**

d) **elimination of Article 2104 obliging member countries in payments crises to follow IMF advice.**

e) **renegotiation of the rules of origin (Chapter Four of NAFTA) to allow governments to require manufacturers to use more local inputs in exported goods.**

These are only some of the needed changes. We have highlighted in particular the need to renegotiate Chapter 11 on Investment because its most negative provisions are precisely the measures that transnational corporations (TNCs) want to incorporate into other international trade agreements.

Under pressure from TNC lobbyists, the European Union has undertaken to persuade other members of the World Trade Organization, the successor to the GATT, to accelerate plans for the renegotiation of the WTO code on Trade-Related Investment Measures (TRIMS). The EU was planning to ask Trade Ministers from WTO member countries to approve a new round of negotiations on investment at their December 1996 meeting in Singapore.

The aim of what the Deputy Director General of the European Commission, Hugo Paemen, calls "an Uruguay Round for investment" is to make the relatively weak TRIMs code into a stronger body of international law with provisions similar to NAFTA's.

Among the specific negotiating objectives set out by the EU is to establish rules guaranteeing investors' freedom to make financial transfers similar to NAFTA Article 1109. The European Commission's document outlining its goals acknowledges the rise of speculative capitalism. It observes that "foreign direct investment to developing countries has quadrupled between 1986 and 1992, whereas **portfolio investment grew 50 times in the same period,** having already reached almost the same level as FDI."[171]

The European Commission acknowledges that some less-developed and Eastern European countries may resist the total liberalization of all capital flows out of concern for "money laundering, destabilizing currency speculation and capital flight."

In fact, an extensive coalition of civic organizations, led by the Third World Network, has organized a campaign to stop the establishment of a multilateral treaty on foreign investment. As Mexico's experience makes clear, any treaty modeled on NAFTA's rules will only benefit footloose capital and set back the goal of regaining democratic control over investment.

B. NATIONAL POLICIES TO REGULATE FINANCE

7. Changes to Bank of Canada Policy

In Chapter Three, we have already discussed several reforms that would allow more democratic control over financial capital in Canada. Here we shall briefly summarize the main conclusions of that analysis.

First of all, it is essential that the federal government appoint Bank of Canada governors who are committed to fulfilling the whole of the Bank's mandate. The Bank of Canada must balance its preoccupation with price stability with an equal concern for job creation and government financial needs. In recent years we have suffered from an exclusive concentration on fighting inflation to the detriment of other policy goals, particularly employment generation.

Second, the Bank of Canada must reclaim more of the policy levers that are at its disposal. The Bank should engineer further reductions in high real interest rates by lowering the target band for overnight rates. The fact that the Bank successfully lowered the overnight rate 17 times over 1995 and 1996 without sparking massive capital flight is encouraging. However, we must keep in mind that these reductions occurred in the context of continuing high unemployment and massive government spending cuts. These short-term interest rate cuts, welcome as they are, do not constitute a change in **monetary policy.**

In order to make an independent monetary policy viable, the Bank of Canada must be prepared to face the possibility that some investors will take their money out of Canada in response to future interest rate cuts. In the past, the Bank of Canada has responded to such private sales of Treasury bills and government bonds by immediately raising interest rates. In Chapter Three we have argued that the Bank has another option: it can instead re-enter the market and purchase Treasury bills and longer-term bonds on its own account.

More active participation by the Bank of Canada in both the short-term and longer-term bond markets would not only help to keep down interest rates. It would also fulfill the policy goal of financing more government debt through Ottawa's own bank where the interest payments ultimately revert to the public treasury.

As explained more fully in the third chapter, the 1996 Alternative Budget suggests; first, a federal requirement that Registered Pension Plans (RPPs) and Registered Retirement Savings Plans (RRSPs) invest a minimum proportion of their portfolios in government bonds as a condition for receiving their tax deductibility; second, a government initiative to gradually lower the ceiling on allowable foreign investments by RPPs and RRSPs; and finally, restoration of the reserve requirements for private financial institutions. Requiring banks, trust companies and other financial institutions to keep a portion of their deposits with the central bank is an important instrument of monetary policy.

While currently there is no threat of renewed inflation from the stimulus afforded by interest rate cuts, reserve requirements are a policy tool that can be used to contain the overall growth of the money supply.

Since the rules were changed in 1991, the private banks have increased their holdings of federal government bonds without having to hold any cash in reserve to back up that debt. The rationale for allowing the banks to hold government bonds without putting up any of their own assets as reserves was a declaration by the Bank for International Settlements that government bonds are "risk-free". This arrangement has been very profitable for the banks, which have added some $50 billion to their holdings of federal debt since 1991.

New reserve requirements can ensure that in the future the Bank of Canada can hold more government debt on its own accounts. Such monetizing of government debt need not be inflationary if the Bank of Canada can at the same time control the growth of the money supply elsewhere by manipulating the amount of reserves the private banks must keep on deposit.

8. Quantitative Controls on Capital Flows

John Maynard Keynes argued that capital controls are necessary so that each country can set its own monetary policy. Referring to his vision for Bretton Woods, Keynes wrote: "We intend to retain control of our domestic rate of interest, so that we can keep it as low as suits our own purposes, without interference from the ebb and flow of international capital movements or flights of hot money... Not merely as a feature of the transition, but as a permanent arrangement, the plan accords to every member-government the explicit right to control capital movements."[172]

The Bretton Woods system explicitly allowed for national controls over capital movements. Canada abandoned these controls relatively early in 1951. Other countries kept them much longer. In 1975, 17 industrial countries and 85 less-developed countries had some type of quantitative restriction on payments for capital transactions. By 1990, 11 industrial countries and 109 less-developed countries had them.[173]

Controls are necessary to prevent tax avoidance by firms who shift assets offshore to avoid paying their share of the social costs engendered by doing business. Capital controls also serve to make room for more domestic control over interest rates. Britain, France and Germany all used capital controls during the 1960s and the 1970s to allow them to keep domestic interest rates below international levels.[174]

James Crotty and Gerald Epstein argue persuasively that "there is no single policy with respect to [capital] controls that is optimal in all countries under all circumstances."[175] They lay out a series of possibilities.

International agreements on capital flight could be negotiated requiring countries to return capital to the government of the country of origin if it crossed borders illegally. Police forces are already calling for closer monitoring of international capital flows to restrict the laundering of drug money. The same monitoring mechanisms could be used to catch other illegal capital flows.

Capital controls can take a number of forms. The most commonly used are quantitative restrictions on the amount of capital that can be transferred across international borders at any one time. To give an idea of the range of possibilities, Crotty and Epstein cite the following examples of the kinds of controls that Ireland had in place in 1992:

- all credits to non-resident Irish-pound-denominated accounts in excess of 250,000 pounds had to be reported to the central bank unless they were trade-related;
- residents were not allowed to make loans in Irish pounds for periods of less than one year to nonresidents without the permission of the central bank;
- there were restrictions on the foreign currency accounts available to residents;
- forward foreign exchange transactions in Irish pounds for speculative purposes were prohibited; and
- all currency swaps required central bank approval.[176]

There is no simple formula for the use of capital controls. Different kinds of controls are appropriate to varied circumstances. Flexibility is needed. However, the historical record clearly shows that they can be effective policy tools.

9. Require Portfolio Investment to Remain for a Minimum Period

One specific example of a particular type of capital control deserves special attention. In Chapter Four we described Chile's law requiring portfolio investment to remain within the country for a minimum of one year.

As noted in Chapter Four, the World Bank's assessment of lessons from the Mexican crisis proposes that ways be found to keep speculative capital under control, while encouraging long-term investment. The World Bank study specifically refers to the success that Chile has had in increasing the share of long-term investment.[177]

The World Bank also notes that Chile is the only country in the Latin America and Caribbean region in which direct investment has predominated over portfolio investment in recent years.[178] However, the Bank fails to point out that one of the major reasons for this success are the Chilean laws regulating foreign investment. Chile requires that foreign investors deposit 30% of the capital they bring into the country with the central bank. Furthermore, foreign portfolio investment must remain within the country for a minimum of one year. Thanks to these laws, Chile was buffeted less than other Latin American countries by the "tequila effect" that destabilized financial markets early in 1995 as nervous investors sought safe havens for their money in the wake of Mexico's troubles.

Laws like those in effect in Chile make eminent sense, not only for less-developed countries, but also for Canada. Unfortunately, in bilateral negotiations with Chile, the Canadian government lined up on the wrong side of this issue. Instead of making an alliance with Chile to defend this type of capital control, the Chrétien government demanded that Chile give up its investment requirements as a condition for signing a bilateral free trade agreement with Canada. To their credit, the Chilean negotiators held out until they won an exemption for their foreign investment rules.

The lack of vision demonstrated by the Canadian negotiators illustrates how the Canada-Chile talks failed to serve Canadian interests. Rather, they were designed to keep alive the prospect of Chilean adhesion to NAFTA during a period when the Clinton administration lacked negotiating authority from Congress.

The Chilean example shows that national governments still can regulate capital flows if they have the tools to do the job. Such laws, however, would not be compatible with the investment provisions of NAFTA, which accordingly must be amended.

It is also doubtful whether such regulation of portfolio capital would be permitted under an extension of the WTO code on Trade-Related Investment Measures as discussed above.

10. Regulate Derivatives

New financial instruments, such as derivatives, have outgrown regulatory regimes designed for an earlier age. For example, since the Great Depression, Canadian and U.S. investors have had their investments protected by deposit insurance. Many commentators argue that, if speculators are going to gamble, they should at least put up their own money and not have their losses guaranteed by the public purse through the Canada Deposit Insurance Corporation or the Federal Deposit Insurance Corporation in the U.S.

Even the editors of the *Financial Times of London* suggest "a two-tier banking system in which the safety net of deposit insurance is denied to commercial banks' derivatives activity."[179]

David Korten[180] makes a number of specific suggestions for regulating derivatives. Pension funds and other funds managed as public trusts should be prohibited from trading in derivatives and from investing in companies that do. Corporations trading in derivatives should be required to report each quarter on the financial exposure to such instruments and reveal the proportion of their trading that involves gambling-grade derivatives.

One way to slow down risky trading would be to eliminate the practice of buying derivatives on margin, insisting that the buyer cover the full purchase price.

C. RESTORE LOCAL CONTROL OVER INVESTMENT CAPITAL

11. Establish Pools of Social Capital

One way to counter the power of footloose speculative capital is to develop pools of investment funds under social control. In our study on *Reweaving Canada's Social Programs,* we propose the establishment of a National Renewal Fund to finance job-creating projects aimed at meeting basic needs.[181] The NRF's other role would be to finance small and medium-sized firms that cannot access bank loans.

The chief means of funding an NRF would be progressive tax reform. For example, if some of the monies raised through the domestic Financial Transfer Tax (FTT) discussed above were dedicated to the NRF, then there would be a direct transfer from speculation into productive investment.

Another underutilized source of capital for social investment is pension funds. Ed Finn estimates that Canadian unionized workers' pension funds now contain more than $360 billion worth of assets. Most of these funds are controlled by trustees appointed by corporate employers, and are not invested in a neutral way, but "tactically, to intimidate, to encourage, to discriminate for or against, to attack, to change or prevent change—in short, to shape a society that conforms to their objectives."

Finn suggests that regaining control over what are really deferred wages earned by workers should be a priority for the unions' leaders. "In a society where clout and influence are measured by the size of the financial club you carry, a policy of letting employers, banks, trust and insurance companies control the biggest accumulation of union members' money—and use it frequently for anti-union purposes—is a policy that keeps the balance of power in labour-management relations tilted decisively in management's favour."[182]

12. Make Banks' Charters Contingent on Social Responsibility

In Canada, private banks operate by virtue of charters issued by Parliament. These charters can be periodically reviewed and their renewal made dependent on how well the banks serve community needs. We already make the renewal of broadcast licenses by the Canadian Radio-television and Telecommunications Commission contingent on performance. A similar system could apply to the banks.

In fact, the revision of the Bank Act in 1997 provides an opportunity to institute measures that would discourage the banks from engaging in speculation and encourage more investment in local communities. So far, in discussing changes to the Bank Act, the news media have focused on disputes over permitting banks into insurance or auto leasing. We need to use the occasion of the revision of the Bank Act for a much deeper debate.

Jordan Grant and George Crowell suggest that we insist that the 1997 revision of the Bank Act reinstate the reserve requirements that were quietly dropped by the Mulroney government in 1991.[183]

Some ideas proposed by bank reform campaigns in the United States merit study with a view to their possible application in Canada. For example, the Financial Democracy Campaign suggests that the renewal of charters be conditional on financial institutions' performance with respect to U.S. laws regarding obligations to reinvest in local communities, provide home mortgages, disclose activities, and extend credit to disadvantaged groups.[184]

U.S. reformers have also called for staggering the income tax rate on earnings from securities according to how long they are held. For example, a 50% rate might be charged on securities held less than six months; 35% on those held six months to three years, and 10% on those held longer than three years.

13. Local Currencies

In their survey of the origins of national currencies, Abraham Rotstein and Colin A. M. Duncan explain how, in ancient, medieval and early modern times, two types of money often co-existed. One currency was used for long-distance trade and another for local transactions. They explain that "The use of distinct monies for the two different spheres helped ensure that traffic in the basics of everyday life was not jeopardized."[185] Even if the money used for international trade, for example, gold or silver, became scarce, the local economy could carry on because its exchanges were settled in local currency.

Rotstein and Duncan are pessimistic about the possibilities of controlling the Euromarket and other kinds of international speculation. Nevertheless, they make an intriguing proposal: "Given that it seems impossible to control international speculation in currencies, the question arises as to the advisability of some contingency planning. Could we moderate a possible disaster by at least partially separating the international and local economies?"[186] They go on to advocate the extension of community-based money systems.

In recent times, several Canadian communities have rediscovered a means of financing local economic activity that was pioneered during the Great Depression. In the Dirty Thirties, people created their own, non-legal tender forms of money. Generally known as "scrip," this do-it-yourself money facilitated self-help economic activity for the unemployed. A local organization would issue tokens to the unemployed either as loans (in the case of desperate need) or as payment for labour. These workers then produced various useful items that were sold, also for tokens. These tokens then could be redeemed at local stores.

Today's experiments are generally known as Local Exchange Trading Systems (LETS). Sometimes the same acronym is used for Local Employment Trading Systems to put an emphasis on their job-creating potential. These community-based trading systems facilitate exchanges of goods and services among individuals and local businesses through the use of locally created currencies. Hundreds of these local currency systems, issuing what are sometimes called "Green Dollars," have been created to supplement the federal money system.

A LETS operation resembles bartering. Mark Hathaway offers the following example: "Pete offers a typing service to Linda, a hairdresser, who pays him in Green Dollars. Pete may then use this money to pay Kathy, a local mechanic who is a member of LETS. Kathy in turn can pay Linda to cut her hair. (Of course, in actual practice, Green Money may circulate through far more hands.)"[187]

An advantage of a LETS system is that the local money recirculates within the community that creates it, sustaining local employment. Hathaway explains how "In the Toronto LETS, members are given an initial 'line of credit' equal to 2,000 Green Dollars (which are considered to have equal value to a regular Canadian dollar.) Unlike regular money, no interest is charged on this amount. In fact, a basic tenet of LETS is that idle money cannot create wealth, only work can...

"No one in the system can profit through speculation. Charging interest on outstanding 'debts' is prohibited because, while interest may be beneficial to investors, it does nothing for the local economy. In LETS, no one is allowed to enrich themselves by leaving money idle. Wealth is seen as something to be shared, not stored."[188]

Most of the participants in LETS are people without much cash but with useful skills. They include single parents, the unemployed, retirees, disabled persons and farmers. Used goods are traded, as well as items that are unavailable, or seldom found on the commercial market, such as organically grown produce.

LETS members are unable to meet all their needs through the network, and so they must also rely on income from the regular economy. Nevertheless, LETS has great potential for supplementing the livelihood of the working poor and the marginally employed. In many LETS transactions there is also a cash component. Typically, a transaction might involve enough cash to cover the cost of externally purchased materials and sufficient green dollars to reimburse the local value added through labour.

These kinds of money offer a limited form of "delinking" from the global and indeed the national monetary order. While green dollars can only be spent in the local community, they offer a high degree of democratic control over the use and management of money. The creation of local currencies is indeed one alternative to the high interest rate, low-income trap of speculative capitalism.

Conclusion: Redirecting Economics from Speculation to Care

The proposals we have offered in this chapter are but the first steps in redirecting economics from a preoccupation with short-term gain for a few to a long-term perspective of care for our common "household." Yet the importance of these steps cannot be underestimated. They could begin to move the economy in fundamentally new directions, and create spaces where even more creative alternatives can emerge. As Manfred Bienefeld writes: "The dream of a caring society can only be kept alive if it is possible to restore a degree of effective national control over the finance sector."[189]

Ultimately, asserting such control over the tides of speculative finance means that we begin to confront this false economy which rewards activities that produce nothing of value, while ignoring those which truly sustain and enhance life. It means we challenge a system that distorts the lives of all who live in it. It means that we begin to free ourselves from the trap of a collective delusion which values money above all else, even if it destroys the very capacity of the planet to sustain life for future generations.

* * * * *

ENDNOTES

1 The Economist Oct. 7, 1995 p.10.

2 calculated from data in ul Haq ed. (1996) The Tobin Tax p.3.

3 Informativo Divida Externa, São Paulo Apr/Mai/Jun 1995 p.11.

4 The Economist Oct. 7, 1995 p.10.

5 cited in CAW Submission to the House of Commons Finance Committee 1994 p.13.

6 calculated from Statistics Canada 13-210-XPB Income after tax, distributions by size in Canada March 1996 Table IV, p.22.

7 UNDP (1996) Human Development Report 1996 p.13.

8 Gorostiaga (1995) "The New Consensus" p.3.

9 Gallardo (1995) "Los Limites del Modelo de Ajuste en América Latina" p.12.

10 Daly, Herman E. and Cobb, John B.(1989) For the Common Good p.38.

11 Third World Resurgence No. 61/62 p.53.

12 Jean Chrétien Notes for an Address to the 14th Annual Plenary of the InterAction Council of Former Heads of State and Government, Vancouver, B.C., May 19, 1996, Ottawa: Office of the Prime Minister, p.1.

13 Ibid. p.5.

14 Ibid. p.3.

15 interview with David Korten in Multinational Monitor Jan.-Feb. 1996 p.26-27.

16 For further analysis of the valuation of women's work, see Marilyn Waring, (1988), If Women Counted.

17 Daly and Cobb (1989) For the Common Good p.138.

18 Ibid. p.138-9.

19 cited in Ralston Saul (1995) The Unconscious Civilization p.130.

20 Rochon (1994) Economics in Crisis p.77.

21 Ibid. p.78.

22 Ibid. p.88.

23 interview with David Korten in Multinational Monitor Jan.-Feb. 1996 p.25

24 Baker et al. "Taxing the Big Casino" The Nation May 9, 1994, p.622.

25 Monthly Review January, 1994 p.17.

26 Korten (1995) When Corporations Rule the World p.196.

27 Bank of Canada Review, Winter 1995-96, p.45.

28 The Economist Oct. 7, 1995, p.9.

29 Korten op. cit. p.196.

30 Ibid. p.198.

31 Financial Times London, Aug. 20, 1996, p.1.

32 Toronto Star June 15, 1996, p.E3.

33 The Globe and Mail Toronto, May 8, 1996, p.B4.

34 CAW Economic and Social Action July, 1995, p.4.

35 The Globe and Mail Toronto, Feb. 5, 1996, p.A10.

36 Working Together: Labor Report of the Americas Minneapolis, Mar.-Apr., 1996, p.5.

37 Statisticas Canada 72-002, Dec. 1995, Table 6.

38 Shaiken and Hertzenberg (1992) Automation and Global Production P.10.

39 Korten op. cit. p.188.

40 Finn (1996) Under Corporate Rule p.68.

41 The Globe and Mail Toronto, Feb. 24, 1996, p.D5.

42 Ibid. July 8, 1996, p.B2.

43 Business Week March 20, 1995, p.47.

44 Finn, op. cit. p.68.

45 Toronto Star March 17, 1996.

46 Business Week March 20, 1995, p.48.

47 cited in The Nation Dec. 6, 1993, p.686.

48 cited in The Globe and Mail Toronto, April 10, 1996, p.B10.

49 Teeple (1995) Globalization and the Decline of Social Reform p.62.

50 Jean Chrétien Notes for an Address to the 14th Annual Plenary of the InterAction Council of Former Heads of State and Government, Vancouver, B.C., May 19, 1996, Ottawa: Office of the Prime Minister, p.3.

51 Martin (1996) Budget Plan, Department of Finance, Ottawa, P.27.

52 The Economist Oct. 7, 1995, p.10.

53 Korten op. cit. p.199.

54 Bank of Canada Review Winter, 1995-96, p.96.

55 CCPA Monitor April 1996, p.8.

56 New York Times Jan. 18, 1995.

57 The Economist Oct. 7, 1995, p.37.

58 Ibid. p.11

59 Bienefeld (1993) "Financial Deregulation: Disarming the Nation State" p.368.

60 The Globe and Mail Toronto, July 6, 1996, p.D5.

61 Statistics Canada 67-202 Table 15.

62 cited in McQuaig (1995) Shooting the Hippo, p.41.

63 DBRS (1995) "The Massive Federal Debt: How Did It Happen?", p.2.

64 Osberg and Fortin (1996) Unnecessary Debts p.33.

65 Ibid. p.71.

66 Stanford (1996) Growth, Interest, and Debt p.1.

67 calculated from Department of Finance (1996) Economic Reference Tables, Table 55, Federal Government Expenditures, National Income and Expenditure Accounts Basis, p.103.

68 Martin (1994) A New Framework for Economic Policy p.83.

69 Martin (1996) Budget Plan, Department of Finance, Ottawa, p.27.

70 Ibid. p.28.

71 Ibid. Table 1.2.

72 Ibid. Table 1.5.

73 Bank of Canada Review, Winter, 1995-96, p.99.

74 Ibid. Summer, 1995, p.57.

75 The Globe and Mail, Toronto, Nov. 28, 1995, B2.

76 CCPA Monitor June, 1995, p.1.

77 Monroy and Peñaloza (1996) Balance Economico 1995 Y Perspectivas para 1996 p.13 & 17.

78 Legler (1995) From Bad to Worse: Neoliberal Restructuring in Mexico Under Salinas and Zedillo P.19.

79 Fortune Sept. 4, 1995, p.98-108.

80 La Jornada Sept. 9, 1995.

81 Burki and Edwards (1995) "Latin America After Mexico" p.6.

82 New York Times Feb. 23, 1995.

83 Warnock (1995) The Other Mexico p.79.

84 Foro de Apoyo Mutuo (1996) Deuda Externa vs Desarrollo Economico p.18.

85 GATT-Fly Report Nov. 1982 "Lessons from Mexico's Crisis".

86 Proceso No. 788 Dec.9, 1991, p.16-21.

87 cited in GATT-Fly Report Nov. 1982, p.1.

88 Moffitt (1983) The World's Money p.196.

89 Ibid. p.196.

90 Wall Street Journal March 27, 1996, p.A4.

91 New York Times April 24, 1995.

92 Legler, op. cit. p.15.

93 Alvarez (1994) "Las privatizaciones en Mexico", p. 26.

94 The Globe and Mail May 22, 1995.

95 Proceso No.758 May13, 1991, p.7.

96 Burki and Edwards, op. cit. p.9.

97 Arroyo (1995) "Hacia un Diagnostico de la Crisis" p.6.

98 RMALC (1996) "Mexico Once Again in Crisis After Two years of NAFTA" p.8.

99 Ibid. p.6.

100 Nadal (1995) "An Alternative Economic Strategy for Mexico" p.4.

101 CAW Economic and Social Action July, 1995, p.6.

102 Financial Times, London, Feb. 22, 1995.

103 La Jornada, Sept. 30, 1995.

104 cited in Financial Times, London, Feb. 16, 1995.

105 Wall Street Journal Jan. 31, 1995.

106 La Jornada June 20, 1995.

107 New York Times Feb. 22, 1995.

108 El Financiero Aug. 20, 1996.

109 Garavito and Manzo (1995) Banca Y Crisis de Pagos p.156.

110 Ibid. p.26.

111 Monroy and Peñaloza op. cit. p.19.

112 Ibid. p.27.

113 Ibid. p.27.

114 RMALC op. cit. p.11.

115 Ibid. p.12.

116 The Other Side of Mexico No. 45, March-April 1996.

117 Proceso No. 1020 May 20, 1996, p.12-19.

118 Toronto Star April 21, 1996, p.B5.

119 Ibid. p.B5.

120 cited in Proceso No. 1020 May 20, 1996, p.19. emphasis added.

121 RMALC op. cit. p.12.

122 The Other Side of Mexico No. 45, March-April 1996, p.5.

123 Garavito and Manzo, op. cit. p.90-92.

124 Ibid. p.132.

125 The Economist Sept. 19, 1992, p.46.

126 Delmaide (1984) Debt Shock p.54.

127 The Economist Sept. 19, 1992, p.10.

128 Helleiner (1995) "Democratic Governance in an Era of Global Finance" p.284.

129 Ibid. p.285.

130 cited in Le Monde Diplomatique May 1995.

131 Moffitt (1983) The World's Money p.20.

132 Epstein (1985) "The Triple Debt Crisis" p.649.

133 Strange (1986) Casino Capitalism p.173.

134 The Globe and Mail May 23, 1996, p.B10.

135 Financial Times, London, Feb. 16, 1995.

136 cited in Michalos (1996) Paying for a Welfare State: The Case for a Tobin Tax p.11.

137 Ibid. p.360.

138 Singer (1993) "The Bretton Woods System: Historical Perspectives" p.13-16.

139 Korten (1995) When Corporations Rule the World p.323.

140 cited in our 1985 book Debt Bondage or Self-Reliance p.81.

141 Wachtel (1986) The Money Mandarins p.208.

142 cited in Michalos op. cit. p.12.

143 see transcript of the talk James Tobin gave at a CCPA seminar May 29, 1995, Canadian Centre for Policy Alternatives, Ottawa, p.7.

144 ul Haq, Mahub et. al. (1996) The Tobin Tax Oxford University Press - hereafter cited as The Tobin Tax..

145 The Tobin Tax p.xvii.

146 cited in Michalos op. cit. p.16.

147 The Tobin Tax p.119.

148 Ibid. p.233.

149 Ibid. p.228.

150 Ibid. Tables 9.2, 9.3 and 9.4 p.238-240.

151 Ibid. p.263.

152 Ibid. p.267.

153 cited in Michalos op. cit. p.7.

154 see Table describing "Transactions Taxes Around the World" in The Tobin Tax p.70.

155 Ibid. p.70.

156 Michalos op. cit. p.8.

157 CCPA Monitor June 1996 p.18.

158 Wachtel op. cit. p.220.

159 Ibid. p.221.

160 Osorio (1996) Deuda Externa Y Alternativas p.11.

161 Monroy and Peñaloza (1996) Balance Economico 1995 Y Perspectivas para 1996 p.5.

162 George (1992) The Debt Boomerang

163 see Osorio (1995) and Foro de Apoyo Mutuo (1995) for full reports on the meeting.

164 Financial Tmes, London, Sept. 30, 1996, p.6.

165 Financial Tmes, London, Sept. 30, 1996, p.16.

166 Mihevc (1996B) Report on the World Bank/IMF Meetings, April 22-24, 1996 p.2.

167 Financial Tmes, London, Sept. 30, 1996, p.16.

168 see our Economic Justice Report Nov. 1995 for a detailed description.

169 see Chapter Seven of our book Recolonization or Liberation.

170 Singer op. cit. p.16.

171 European Commission (1995) Objectives and Contents of the European Commission Initiative for Establishing International Rules for Foreign Investments p.9.

172 cited in The Economist Sept. 19, 1992 p.10.

173 Crotty and Epstein (1996) "In Defence of Capital Controls" p.141.

174 Ibid. p.143.

175 Ibid. p.136.

176 Ibid. p.141.

177 Burki and Edwards (1995) "Latin America After Mexico" p.6.

178 Ibid. p.9.

179 Financial Times London Dec. 30, 1994.

180 Korten (1995) When Corporations Rule the World p.314.

181 ECEJ (1993) Reweaving Canada's Social Programs p.59.

182 Finn (1996) Under Corporate Rule p.68.

183 Canadian Perspectives Summer 1996 p.15.

184 Barnet and Cavanagh (1994) Global Dreams p.417.

185 Drache and Gertler (1991) The New Era of Global Competition p.419.

186 Ibid. p.422.

187 Hathaway (1996) "Re-inventing Economics... Creating Community" p.21.

188 Ibid. p.22.

189 Bienefeld (1993) "Financial Deregulation: Disarming the Nation State" p.348.

BIBLIOGRAPHY

Alvarez, Alejandro (1994) "Las privatizaciones en Mexico, 1988-1994: economia politica de la fabricación de millionarios", paper presented at Laval University, Quebec City. Alejandro Alvarez is an economist at the Universidad Nacional Autonoma de Mexico, Mexico City.

Arroyo, Alberto (1995) "Hacia un Diagnostico de la Crisis y Propuesta de Condiciones Minimas para Enfrentarla", Cuernavaca: unpublished.

Baker, Dean; Poulin, Robert; and Schaberg, Marc (1994) "Taxing the Big Casino" The Nation May 9, p.622-624.

Barnet, Richard and Cavanagh, John (1994) Global Dreams: Imperial Corporations and the New World Order New York: Simon and Shuster.

Burki, Shahid Javed and Edwards, Sebastian (1995) Latin America After Mexico: Quickening the Pace Washington: The World Bank.

Bienefeld, Manfred (1993) "Financial Deregulation: Disarming the Nation State" in Jenson, J., Mahon, R. and Bienefeld, M., eds. Production, Space, Identity: Political Economy Faces the 21st Century Toronto: Canadian Scholars' Press.

Boyer, Robert and Drache, Daniel (1996) States Against Markets: The Limits of Globalization London and New York: Routledge.

Cameron, Duncan and Finn, Ed (1996) 10 Deficit Myths: The Truth About Government Debts and Why They Don't Justify Cutbacks Ottawa: Canadian Centre for Policy Alternatives.

Chan, Michelle (1996) The Anatomy of a DEAL: A Handbook on International Project Finance Washington: Friends of the Earth.

Chrétien, Jean, Notes for an Address to the 14th Annual Plenary of the InterAction Council of Former Heads of State and Government Vancouver, B.C., May 19, 1996, Ottawa: Office of the Prime Minister.

Crotty, James and Epstein, Gerald "In Defence of Capital Controls" in Panitch, Leo, ed. (1996) Are There Alternatives? The Socialist Register 1996 Halifax: Fernwood

DBRS (1995) "The Massive Federal Debt: How Did It Happen?" Toronto: Dominion Bond Rating Service.

CAW (1994) Submission to the House of Commons Standing Committee on Finance North York: Canadian Auto Workers.

Daly, Herman E. and Cobb, John B. (1989) For the Common Good: Redirecting the Economy toward Community, the Environment, and a Sustainable Future Boston: Beacon Press.

Delmaide, Darrell, (1984) Debt Shock Toronto: Lester & Orpen Denys.

Drache, Daniel and Gertler, Meric (1991) The New Era of Global Competition: State Policy and Market Power Montreal & Kingston: McGill-Queen's University Press.

ECEJ (1990) Recolonization or Liberation: The Bonds of Structural Adjustment and Struggles for Emancipation Toronto: Ecumenical Coalition for Economic Justice.

ECEJ (1993) Reweaving Canada's Social Programs: From Shredded Safety Net to Social Solidarity Toronto: Ecumenical Coalition for Economic Justice.

Epstein, Gerald (1985) "The Triple Debt Crisis" World Policy Vol. II, No. 4. New York: World Policy Institute.

European Commission (1995) Objectives and Contents of the European Commission Initiative for Establishing International Rules for Foreign Investments Brussels: European Commission.

Finn, Ed (1996) Under Corporate Rule: The Big Business Takeover of Canada Ottawa: Canadian Centre for Policy Alternatives.

Foro de Apoyo Mutuo (1996) Deuda Externa vs Desarrollo Economico: Analisis y Sintesis de la Reunion Internacional Sobre Deuda Externa y Alternativas, Mexico City: Foro de Apoyo Mutuo.

Gallardo, Helio (1995) "Los límites del modelo de ajuste en América Latina" en América Latina: Los Límites del Ajuste y sus Alternativas, Santiago: REDLAC.

Garavito, Rosa Albina and Manzo, Jose Luis (1985) Banca y Crisis de Pagos: Hacia Una Solucion Integral Mexico City: Instituto de Estudios de la Revolucion Democratica.

GATT-Fly (1982) "Lessons from Mexico's Crisis" GATT-Fly Report Toronto. GATT-Fly is the former name of the Ecumenical Coalition for Economic Justice.

GATT-Fly (1985) Debt Bondage or Self-Reliance: A Popular Perspective on the Global Debt Crisis Toronto: GATT-Fly.

George, Susan (1992) The Debt Boomerang: How Third World Debt Harms Us All Boulder: Westview Press.

Gorostiaga, Xabier (1995) "The New Consensus: A Civilization Based on Harmony and Simplicity" paper presented to the Conference "New Development Options", Oslo.

Hathaway, Mark (1996) "From Death to Life: Revisioning Economics" and "Re-inventing Economics..Creating Community" in Scarboro Missions Vol. 77 No. 3, Scarboro Foreign Mission Society.

Helleiner, Eric (1995) "Democratic Governance in an Era of Global Finance" in Cameron, Maxwell and Appell Mott, Maureen, eds. Democracy and Foreign Policy: Canada Among Nations 1995 Ottawa: Carlton University Press.

Kapstein, Ethan (1996) "Workers and the World Economy" Foreign Affairs Vol. 75, No. 3, May/June p.16-37.

Korten, David C. (1995) When Corporations Rule the World West Hartford: Kumarian.

Laurell, Asa Cristina (1996) No Hay Pierde: Todos Pierden: Lo que usted necesita saber sobre la nueva ley del Seguro Social Mexico City: Instituto de Estudios de la Revolución Democrática.

Legler, Thomas (1995) From Bad to Worse: Neoliberal Restructuring in Mexico Under Salinas and Zedillo Toronto: Canada-Americas Policy Alternatives.

Laxer, James (1993) False God: How the Globalization Myth Has Impoverished Canada Toronto: Lester.

Martin, Paul (1994) A New Framework for Economic Policy Ottawa: Department of Finance.

Martin, Paul (1996) Budget Plan Ottawa: Department of Finance.

McQuaig, Linda (1995) Shooting the Hippo: Death by Deficit and Other Canadian Myths Toronto: Viking.

Michalos, Alex C. (1996) Paying for a Welfare State: The Case for a Tobin Tax paper presented to the annual meeting of the B.C. Political Science Assotiation, Prince George, British Columbia.

Mihevc, John (1996A) Multilateral Debt Reduction: A Proposed Framework Toronto: Inter-Chruch Coalition on Africa.

Mihevc, John (1996B) Report on World Bank/IMF Meetings April 22-24, 1996 Toronto: Inter-Church Coalition on Africa.

Moffitt, Michael (1983) The World's Money: International Banking from Bretton Woods to the Brink of Insolvency New York: Simon and Schuster.

Monroy Gómez, Mario and Peñaloza Méndez, Andrés (1996) Balance Economico 1995 Y Perspectivas para 1996, Mexico City: Red Mexicana de Acción Frente al Libre Comercio and Servicios Informativos Procesados.

Nadal Egea, Alejandro (1995) An Alternative Economic Strategy for Mexico: A Commentary Mexico City: Secretariat of the Liberty Referendum.

Naylor, R.T. (1987) Hot Money and the Politics of Debt Toronto: McClelland and Stewart.

Osberg, Lars and Fortin, Pierre (1996) Unnecessary Debts Toronto: Lorimer.

Osorio, Victor; and Medina, Javier ed. (1995) Deuda Externa Y Alternativas Mexico City: Red Mexicana de Accion Frente al Libre Comercio.

Ralston Saul, John (1995) The Unconscious Civilization Concord: Anansi.

Rifkin, Jeremy (1995) The End of Work: The Decline of the Global Labour Force and the Dawn of the Post-Market Era New York: Putnam.

RMALC (1994) Integración, Democracia Y Desarrollo: Hacia Una Agenda Social Continental Mexico City: Red Mexicana de Acción Frente al Libre Comercio.

RMALC (1996) "Mexico: Once Again in Crisis After Two Years of NAFTA" report prepared for the conference Challenging 'Free Trade' in the Americas: Building Common Responses, sponsored by the Canadian Labour Congress, Ottawa, March 1996.

Rochon, Louis-Philippe (1994) Economics in Crisis Montreal: Robert Davies.

Shaiken, Harley and Hertzenberg, Stephen (1992) Automation and Global Production: Auto Engine Production in Mexico, the US and Canada San Diego: Centre for U.S.-Mexico Studies, University of California.

Singer, Hans W. (1993) "The Bretton Woods System: Historical Perspectives" Third World Economics 16 - 31 August, p.13-16.

Stanford, Jim (1996) Growth, Interest, and Debt: Canada's Fall from the Fiscal Knife-Edge Alternative Federal Budget 1996, Technical Paper #2, Ottawa: Canadian Centre for Policy Alternatives.

Teeple, Garry (1995) Globalization and the Decline of Social Reform Toronto: Garamond.

ul Haq, Mahbub; Kaul, Inge; and Grunberg, Isabelle eds. (1996) The Tobin Tax: Coping with Financial Volatility Oxford: Oxford University Press.

UNDP (1992 and 1996) Human Development Report New York: Oxford University Press.

Wachtel,Howard (1986) The Money Mandarins: The Making of a Supranational Economic Order New York: Pantheon.

Waring, Marilyn (1988) If Women Counted San Francisco: Harper.

Warnock, John (1995) The Other Mexico: The North American Triangle Completed Montreal: Black Rose.

Periodicals:

Bank of Canada Review Ottawa

Business Week

Canadian Perspectives Ottawa: The Council of Canadians

CCPA Monitor Ottawa: Canadian Centre for Policy Alternatives

Economic and Social Action, North York: Canadian Auto Workers

Economic Justice Report Toronto: Ecumenical Coalition for Economic Justice

Economic Justice Update Toronto: Inter-Church Coalition on Africa

Economic Reform Toronto: Committee on Monetary and Economic Reform

The Economist London UK

Financial Times London

The Globe and Mail, Toronto

Informativo Divida Externa, São Paulo

La Jornada Mexico City

Le Monde Diplomatique Paris

Multinational Monitor

Monthly Review

New York Times

The Other Side of Mexico Mexico City: Equipo Pueblo
Proceso Mexico City

Toronto Star

Third World Resurgence Penang

Wall Street Journal

Working Together: Labor Report of the Americas
Minneapolis: Resource Center of the Americas

Internet Information Sources:

Analysis Mexico City: Equipo Pueblo

Heartbeat of Mexico Mexico City: Fronteras Comunes

Mexpaz Mexico City: Servicios Informativos Procesados (SIPRO)

NOTES

NOTES

NOTES

NOTES

NOTES

25 Buying derivatives "on margin"